AS IF

I Had a Life

A memoir of a mom, wife, and
somewhat of a person

Maxine Parrick

Written by Maxx Parrick

Cover Illustration by Morgan S. Parrick

Design by Illumination Graphics

IBSN: 978-0-9828-448-2-2

Dedication

*A big "Thank You" to that Husband Person,
and to Things # 1 and #2.*

*You proved that not only is a family survivable,
it's super fun.*

*Special thanks to "Baby Rosie" who's made my transition
into an Older More Mature Woman, a lot easier!*

Table of Contents

PROLOGUE

Wait a Minute, Who Am I???

I'VE WRITTEN A "SEXY ROMANTIC COMEDY." You'd be surprised how many people raise their tattooed eyebrows up at that news. I'm sure it's an issue of good credentials or at least, related experience. After all, I am known as a *Mother;* therefore, it is unlikely that I could have any experience in *another kind* of life—one that involves sex. As if!

Well, some may not think that romance and great sex is my forte, but craziness and zany experiences—hell, I am *the* expert. This book should prove that, I may appear at times to be sexless, but I do have humor—sick humor, which ninety percent of the time involves something prurient, but humor all the same. I'm finally doing what my friends, husband and kids have told me to do. Well sort of. They told me to do stand-up comedy. I figure that

AS IF I HAD A LIFE

I've stood up enough for those people and I'd just as soon sit on my fat ass, thank you. Besides, I have varicose veins, so standing is painful. My feet also hurt, so forget any vertical business. I am *writing* about what's funny. Because according to them (especially my daughters) I'm really, *really* funny. Now sometimes when they tell me this, it is accompanied by that double eye-roll thing, (more about that *later,)* but I like to think they are sincere.

Having children can be pretty damn amusing. Well, at least *I* became hilarious, accompanied by, *delirious.* Let's face it; we need a good laugh like a gulp of Xanax at least two times a day. And I know that you all have a funny bone out there somewhere that needs to be nudged, and girlfriends, I'm your nudger. I am looking for my mommy-sisters. You know who you are. You are *not* perfect size four. You are way past forty, maybe even in the middle of the fearless fifties. You could even be into your pioneering sixties, bless you. I reach out to those who look at their thighs every morning and wonder how they could transfer the fat to the starving millions or at least to their nasal-basal smile lines.

I want to talk to that mommy who is forced to wear a hideous over-sized, unflattering, neon green T-shirt that proclaims she is the proud mother of "Laurie" or "Robert" and so on. We all know that she is wearing the dreadful garment while a perfectly lovely morning ebbs away as she watches one tedious soccer game after another. And she does this, *every damn Saturday.* Or it's a swim meet, or a boat race, or a hockey game, or base-ball. You get my drift, I am sure. While she smiles, cutting endless oranges for a healthy snack, you know she vaguely remembers when Saturday afternoons were for lazy lovemaking or even better, a mani-pedi. I speak to the Mom who after suffering the humiliation of being seen in what amounts to a large lumpy duvet, embroidered with a purple soccer ball that sinks between one's boobs, drives eight wild children to the Burger King. Once there, she will spend $57.00 on food that is guaranteed to help her fill out the shirt for sure.

I am writing to all the mommies who survived the media blitz, the cheer leading from Gloria Steinman to Tipper Gore. You've endured the "natural" aging of Cindy Crawford, Tyra Banks, and Merle Streep. You brave souls, who still have hope, hence you still try to read: Vogue, Vanity Fair, The New Yorker, whilst reviewing endless homework assignments and writing checks for yet another fund-raiser. I am talking to you, you outrageous ladies who have to be cool and the dispenser of "tough love" to the same kids at the same time.

And let us not forget that you need to be a sex goddess as well. As you hover on the toilet, for your illegal fifteen minutes of alone time, clutching your worn copy of <u>Fifty Shades of Grey</u> to your trembling, falling boobs, I'm seeking you out. Yes, all of you confused, dazed and dazzling *real* women, without access to personal chefs, daily makeup artists–real mommies. My goal is to get an "Oh, Jeez, that happened to me too!" accompanied by a chuckle. I don't ask for more than a chuckle because the Botox might make an outright smile or laugh impossible or painful. Therefore, I will accept a grimace.

You see, I finally figured out that it is all about *The Love*. You fall into it, you make it, and then you produce creatures that suck it up with a ravenous appetite, while you clamor for a way, and ask yourself, *why*, to give them more. Eventually you get it back: more love, and if you're lucky enough to be a grandparent: *revenge.*

CHAPTER ONE

Reality Hurts, Even with Lamaze

Yes, it's all about The Love.
However, it starts with the Big Lie.
You know which one.

REMEMBER WHEN THEY (THE KNOW-IT-ALL-DOCTOR and that bright-eyed nurse practitioner), told you that, there is such a thing as *Natural Childbirth*. I mean *really*, whom are they kidding? I ask you, have you *looked* down there? Come on girls, here in the 21st century, we're supposed to be very OK with peaking in on our "little friend" (I gave mine my middle name, "Frances" I personally never cared for the name, but thought my pubic area might like it.) Anyway, it's pretty damn small "down there." Frankly I still don't understand why one is expected to shoot an eight pound, eleven once anything out, and then have the audacity to call it *natural.*

Shopping at Nordstrom's, that's *natural.* Buying three pairs of shoes, (more about that later) *that* is natural. But blowing up forty-five pounds, watching my size seven feet grow like an alien attachment to size nines–that's just damn unnatural and well, *indignant.* I mean I kept getting bigger and bigger, and in the case of daughter number two, I also threw-up the whole time, but somehow managed to gain over fifty pounds, making me the most unsuccessful bulimic on the planet. My feet were having their own "natural" experience; they grew little "baby feet" under my toes. When I'd look down (and that was a major effort, believe me) I'd see these pudgy, duck-feet with pregnant toes that now were visible twenty-four-seven because no shoes but flip-flops fitted my feet.

I notice now that the celebrities and help us, the other "normal" young moms-to-be are wearing clingy, and belly exposing tops and bottoms. Apparently, they are proud to proclaim their protruding tummies. Of course, most of those young women start off as size ones, so a teeny tiny dodge-ball size stomach is manageable and unlike me, their asses didn't grow to the size of a medicine ball either. Well, good for you my darlings. Not me. My navel popped out like a malformed penis. It was not a pretty sight. I mean *I* didn't want to look at it, yet alone force the world to stare.

When I'd go in for the check up my OBGYN nurse would shake her head and chuckle, "My, we've got quite a little flag marker on this hill, now don't we?" I wasn't sure which part of my anatomy she was referring too. Was she saying the baby was a *boy*? No, she wasn't discussing my *internal* picture. Turns out it was my stand-at-attention-naval. Her sense of humor was tasteless to say the least. I really don't know what she found so damn funny; she told me that she had *birthed* (and those were her words, as if she had dropped a litter) *four* kids. Maybe her navel just sunk inside her. I understand now, that the mommy millennials wouldn't be caught dead without their designer drugs, for a faux-natural childbirth experience. It's really is great that times have changed. Some things will not, no matter how cute the designer maternity clothes.

"Lamaze training program in natural childbirth, emphasizing breathing control and relaxation during labor together with the presence and encouraging assistance of the labor coach ...without the use of drugs."

Labor? Where was my union rep to help me out? I mean I was for sure, under duress during my endurance performance. *Natural* childbirth. There I was, puffing and wanting to scream, but my husband who had taken the coaching classes, wanted me to *exhale.* I think that would be fine if it could be accompanied by a brutal ear-popping scream. It was very un-PC to scream; one was allowed to "ah-hee," but no guttural moans or high pitch cries were allowed. I was to refrain from screaming that my husband was a "bastard" or calling the labor nurse a heartless bitch.

My first child sucked me in so to speak. For an unnatural event, she was a fairly easy pregnancy. I sailed through gestation, barely gaining 25 lbs. I ran until the day I went into labor, and then, let me tell you that at the onset of her birth, the whole gig was a set-up. My first born showed me a basic personality flaw from day one as she resisted her way down the birth canal. She just wasn't going to come out upon request, even when my husband, aka "Coach" and I waited ever so patiently, yes, even welcoming the excruciating cramps that would, according to the birthing class handout, "joyfully hail the onset of the birthing process."

I squeaked out a pitiful cry-for-help, "Pain! Pain!"

"Yes, this is good." Dr. Death clapped his hands with glee. "We will give you some meds now."

"Oh, thank God," I exhaled, waiting for my drug-induced euphoria of child-birthing to set in.

However, apparently, they were not excruciating enough, so the doctor, Dr. Harvey-Death-Will-Be-A-Relief-After-This-Goldstein, gave me the wonder drug "Pitsosin". I asked again for pain meds, he pointed out that I wasn't at "that stage" yet. What stage? The bends stage? The wish-I-were-dead stage? No, I needed to show some real *progress* in dilation. He assured us that this would hasten the process. I was in a haze of pain, paws up so to speak, so I relented. *Faster was better, right?*

Now this drug I'm pretty sure probably was invented as tool for undercover interrogation, because let me tell you, you will say or do anything to make that stuff stop. For those of you who somehow skipped that experience, Pitocin accelerates labor. In other words, you go from *Phase One* to well, *Out the Shoot—please!* All the while you're riding on the most wrenching cramps you can think of. Now the professional-pain-dispensers call this phase, "Transitional Labor." I assume that's because you are transitioning to Hell. On the old pain-scale of one through ten, these cramps are a clear twelve.

Just about the time that I had my first semi-fainting spell from pain and/or exhaustion, my husband, oops, I mean my *coach*, declared that he was "a wreck" and needed a break from his job, cheer-leading. First, he adjusted his baseball cap embroidered with the word "Coach" in blood red on the brim, then he disappeared to "replenish" himself. There I am, hooked up to my own special replenishment: the IV-of-terror.

Fifteen minutes passed, and I was now back on the nasty ride on the Highway of Cramps and in toddled my beloved, clutching a big juicy rare hamburger that he thoughtfully ate in the corner chair. I was desperately trying to remember about *The Love*. But it was very hard, ladies, very, very hard. Between his gulps of barely cooked flesh, I alerted him that I was in the midst of another contraction. Even though I was panting like a dog left in a mini-van, he had to confirm my pain by checking that helpful monitor that lets me know that my insides were about to explode.

"Here Sweetie, let me help you." He popped out of his chair, (never once letting go of his Biggaburger,) and attempted to *coach* me into singing the "a-heeing" song.

At last, I had no choice but to tell him to shut-the-fuck up and get me some heroin. He countered with a firm reminder that *we* were going natural and that *we* are breathing. I replied by grabbing his private parts and asking him to try breathing through *that*. Once he scraped his burger off the floor, and got over the special tingling feeling in his testicles, he brilliantly got the idea.

He looked at me in total shock and frowned, "Don't you want to continue with the Lamaze? I thought you wanted to do it the right way?"

"The *right* way?" I snarled at him as I blew sweat-matted hair out of my mouth and hissed, "Fuck you and this whole thing. *You* have this baby, I'm out of here!" Of course, I was just raving, as my legs were up in the air, and I had nothing on but the lovely pink and blue do-it-yourself gown and an IV in my hand. Clearly, I was going nowhere, but it felt good to take it out on my poor husband.

I'm sorry, but the breathing thing proved to be just crap, at least for me. "Focusing" was crap. The only thing that wasn't crap was the great pain drug that I finally got. Now those were, in the words of my now-grown-up-daughters, "awesome."

Once it was over, I promised myself that I'd let go of all those hateful thoughts—oh wait, it's been what, thirty years and I still can remember? Well, let's face it, that's one event (or two, or three or God-help-you, more) that you will *never* forget. How could anyone possibly have known what having a baby is like? Do you seriously think our mothers would ever tell us the *Truth*? If they did, no one would ever get pregnant. The pain of childbirth finally explains why my mom would sometimes glare at me for no apparent reason. I thought it was because I'd dyed my hair pink: no, she was *remembering*.

Now don't misjudge me here. I love having the baby—as in, *afterwards*. It is great once the baby is born. I felt a euphoric high. Yep, there must be some mighty powerful hormones that flood our bodies, because "the miracle of birth" clouds your wimpy mind and you *almost* forget the pain. Right? Clearly, we all do, otherwise the world would be filled with single children. Well, there *is* that cute little episiotomy to remind you. You know that beatific smile you see on women as they walk by pushing their baby strollers? That's because they have a secret.; they are the ones who had the doctor sew that hole *completely* up.

Of course, horny husbands do not quite grasp this. Normally my husband is a sensitive guy, but the no-entry-depravation finally warped his character. He actually kept a "Getting-My-Wife Laid-Count-Down" calendar. He didn't even have the class to keep it in his office—it was pasted to our bathroom mirror. Every time I went to the restroom, winced in pain, I glared at that paper and planned my revenge. So cute, those little X's marking the magic *six* weeks. For him it was ten—punishment for the burger *and* that damn calendar. I figured that was a discount compared to the twelve hours of labor.

Following the birth of the first child (whom I lovingly refer to as "Thing One" to protect her from the lifetime embarrassment of acknowledging that I am indeed, her mother), I could hardly wait to come home. In fact, I demanded to be discharged early. I wised up by the second child. They had to bring a written order and a security guard to I escort my sorry ass out. By that second birth, I understood that the spa-like birthing facility provided the only sleep, food and attention I'd be getting for the next two years.

Let me return to the Thing One experience. She was nursed, loved, changed and coddled, but did not show much appreciation for any of it. She pretty much spent her first three weeks screaming her brains out. The pediatrician diagnosed the problem as "colic" which means that the poor baby had gas and will be screaming her brains out. Which actually helped her release the gas. Who knew?

I admit that this was a tough time. I was a college instructor who'd taught Child Development courses and here I was re-living every piece of bullshit I'd ever said. I have more to add about that in the next few chapters. Let's just say that *talking* about parenting is way easier than *being* one, and people who think they know it all should just, well, shut the fuck up. All that holds it together is love.

And I admit it: Some days, nights, early mornings, well, it takes a truckload.

CHAPTER TWO

Laundry-folding Techniques in a Mini-Van and other Opportunities for Personal Growth

FIRST, LET ME SAY, THOSE BABY YEARS REALLY ARE GREAT and they go way too fast. I loved being a mommy and utilized all my education, my Master's Degree and my five credentials, to make every moment of my children's lives a fabulous learning experience. Unfortunately, I had a few things to learn myself: *most of that shit is useless.*

One notable experience was when Thing One finished the colicky thing and went on to the teething thing. Every tooth was agony for her, and hellish for me. She cried, she spiked a fever, she vomited, and she drooled. I took her into her pediatrician. How many mommies wanted to secretly sleep with their child's' doctor because he's the *only one* in the world telling you what a good mom you are, how right you are, how you're doing great and looking great? I told him that Thing One's great grandma suggested dipping my finger in whiskey and coating her inflamed gums.

"Does that work?" I asked plaintively.

Doctor Goodeeds nodded. "Yup." He was a man of few words.

"How do I do it? Do I use my finger or a cotton swap?" I was in earnest now. I wanted to be a good mother. I wanted the toddler to stop hurting. *I wanted to run away.*

"Well, you pour a shot in a shot glass," he raised his brows, "and you can stick your finger in there. Go all around the gum line. And then…" He turned and gave me a big smirk, "you drink the rest. You won't give a shit if she's crying or not."

I still love that guy.

My first reality check on parenting actually happened when I returned to part time teaching at the local community college, just six weeks after the birth of Thing One. I was teaching Child Development. I was thrilled to be back, and expected it to be a slam-dunk. After all I had the same lesson plan as before and now I was a true parent. I *really* knew it all! My joy was short-lived. I began by greeting my students and embarked on an overview of the syllabus. Someone in the back snickered. Another, a student who had taken previous classes with me, looked up at me with an anxious frown.

I glared at her. "Is there something you want to add Marcie?"

"Err… Ms. M, uh what you just said didn't make any sense."

"Well," I puffed out my newly huge nursing boobs and sucked in my destroyed belly, "once you review the materials…" Only, as it turns out, that was *not* what I was saying.

Apparently, what I said was, " Go bobblyduh…. Err… syall-a-bus…dah…duh." I was babbling incoherently. Had I had a stroke? No, just a baby. I came to realize that the placenta as it's exiting your body, pulls out your brain tissue. That along with nursing eighteen times a day, no sleep and jamming food in your mouth when you can, can lead to some pretty fucked-up word explosions and some fuzzy thinking skills.

It was a rough first hour. I took a break, drank some coffee and took deep cleansing breaths.

My students included future teachers, parents and even nursing students. It was just such a student who gave me a life-long lesson in the reality of parenting. "Sally" was a student nurse and also the mother of five children–two girls and three boys. That alone was enough to send a normal woman running away. She solved the problem by going to school at night and working the swing shift at a nearby hospital, cleverly avoiding the darlings during their waking hours. Obviously, she had not avoided her *husband* since he'd managed to get her knocked up five times. At any rate, Sally and I were having an on-going little dispute regarding child rearing.

You see, I was lecturing about "Alternative Forms of Discipline" namely, avoiding physical discipline, affectionately known as "spanking." Of course, I had all the answers. After all, Thing One was a darling infant of nine months and I did have

Master's Degree and *five* credentials–I knew it all and I was in fact *The Instructor*. However, Sally, upon hearing me suggest, "Just explain that it is not okay to throw the ball in the house," burst into laughter. Rude laughter followed by her mumbling not-so-under-her-breath, "Bull Shit."

Let me add, that the above epithet was said with a drawling Southern accent, making it a very effective insult, indeed.

Annoyed, I confronted her, "And just what would *you* do?"

Sally chuckled and reached inside her purse, a sly knowing smirk stretched her face. "Well Sugar," she drawled (she was from Texas), "When I want my children to do *anything*, I just show them this."

She proceeded to pull out of her bag, a hairbrush big enough to groom a horse. The entire class gasped and then, damn them, started cheering! I was humiliated. After all, *I* was the one with the *Master's degree and five credentials*. How dare she try to undermine my wisdom? So what if my child was still an adorable little infant? I had all the answers; I was the goddamn *instructor*.

Incensed, I began a vigorous lecture about the dangers of physical force and even though Sally continued to argue with me, I felt that I had prevailed. After all, I was the one who really knew everything—just ask me. And although Sally got a much deserved "A", I continued as a highly-committed college instructor, all semester, to try and change her mind. Yet, something inside nagged at me. I wondered if just maybe, she might be right? Could I someday wind up resorting to *violence* against my precious child? *Ridiculous*, I thought, as I gazed down into her sweet innocent blue eyes.

Then, Thing One turned two. Because I had a Master's degree and five credentials, even a simple trip to the market was viewed as an opportunity to open Thing One's world to knowledge. Therefore, what should have taken only thirty minutes, often took ninety. Why? Because I'd explain every dicky-la-la thing to my twenty-four-month-old child.

"See the peas? Peas grow in a pod! What color are the peas? Yummy, peas. They are such a good vegetable." I'd drone on and on, rambling on about the radishes, the broccoli, and the farmer who grew the food. Then I'd move on to note the colors of the store, the wheels of the shopping cart. I thought I was imparting vast knowledge, what I *was* doing, was boring my child to madness, or at least, over-whelming her with a deluge of meaningless information. And soon, as any e*xperienced* mother would have told me, had I listened, my toddler gave *me* a real lesson in parenting. As it is with many of life's lessons, it was cruel, it was harsh, it was ugly.

Sadly, I *really* thought that I was an expert in Child Development. After all, I had that Master's Degree and Five Credentials. So, I knew everything. I didn't let Thing One's restlessness bother me. I simply lifted her out of the shopping cart so she could "explore" her environment. Of course, I didn't notice how annoyed those around me were when my child began eating the radishes off the display–I simply picked her up, firmly reminding her that *this* food was for observing only, not eating. Puzzled, Thing One hunkered down into the seat and glared at her dumb mother.

The incident repeated itself several times, which of course, extended what was quickly becoming a vastly painful experience. Thing One continued to whine, I continued to cave in for "learning sake." Once out of the seat again, her yammering got louder and suddenly stood up and took off, careened around the aisles. At one point, she tripped a little old lady dragging one of those private carts. I just scooped up my darling, with a gentle "reminder" that it was not "OK" to bump the nice lady, and plopped my child back into the shopping cart seat.

Suddenly, Thing One had let out a yelp that sounded strangely like a war-whoop. At the same time, she did this amazing thing: she catapulted herself out of the shopping cart! I mean it–*she levitated right out*. Oh, except for her shoe–it got wedged between the seat and the side railing. So, visualize that the two-year-old was hanging sideways out of the Safeway shopping cart, while her little body writhed its way south. Oh, did I mention she had started screaming like a banshee? I however, remained calm. I remained *The Perfect Mother*.

I also chose to ignore small crowd of by-standers, who I heard hissing under their breaths, "Some parents should get a license before they have kids."
The nerve of those people. *Didn't they know that I had a graduate degree and those damn credentials?* I inhaled a deep calming breath and leaned over as I eased my toddler down until she gently slid to the filthy floor.

Remembering my child development guidelines, I lowered myself into an attractive squat, so I could be at the mini-monster's eye level.

"Thing One?" I gently whispered, "It is not alright to jump out of the cart. You could have gotten hurt. And now, you are lying on the nasty germ-infested floor and someone might step on you."

My daughter glared at me, ran her baby pudgy hand along the dirty floor and promptly stuck three fingers of the same hand into her mouth. Then she growled, "No Mommy. Stupid mommy."

Can you believe it? She called *me* stupid. Me with my *Master's degree* and those *FIVE credentials*? I was still the professional. I was still in control. "Thing One, honey, it's not okay to call Mommy 'stupid.' Those are mean words and I know you are sorry. So, let's get back into the seat and get those yummy fish sticks from the sea!" I cheerfully reached out and scooped her up into my arms. I looked around sheepishly to the crowd surrounding me. I nodded, *see, I have it all under control, you bitches.*

And *that's* when I needed an exorcist. My darling baby became the Evil Chucky Doll. With a deft twist that would defy any yoga teacher, she jumped out of my grasp and went flying back down to the floor. She landed with a thump and then started screeching and wailing, "Noooooooooooooooo! Bad mommy! Bad Mommy! Mean Mommy! No shop! Go home!"

The surrounding audience gasped in unison. My credibility was on the line now, I remembered how often I had told my students that if one's child had a temper tantrum in the store, simply "pack up your purse, grab your child and go home. Avoid subjecting those around you to your child's screaming. Don't worry about those groceries."

Well, I can tell you that there was no way in hell I was going to tank ninety minutes and a hundred and ten dollars' worth of groceries just to relieve those around me of Thing One's screaming. Instead I crouched down and snarled, "Thing One–you need to stop this right now!"

Right on cue, Thing One snapped back, "No!" and then she spat a full load of baby mucus blended in with hijacked broccoli, along with a cranberry nut granola bar right onto my baby blue sweater. Now I can put up with embarrassment but a five-dollar cleaning bill is just over the top for me. I grabbed her cute little pudgy arm and snarled, "If you don't stop this right now I'm going to *kill* you!" Now that's a child-development approach, all right.

Mind you, I didn't threaten *a spanking*–oh no, I was ready to go to jail instead. But my career and my daughter's life were saved by the sing-song and oh-so-smug voice of former-student Sally who purred behind me, "Do you need this?"

There it was: *The Brush.* I turned and there she stood, with the *"Instrument of Respect and Corporal Punishment"* in her hand. I'm surprised her face didn't crack from that knowing grin. I hung my head in shame and mumbled, "No thank you. I have a Master's degree and five credentials and I think I'm going home now."

Having sensed her mother's defeat, Thing One had stopped her screaming, sat up and opened her arms wide for her loving mommy to pick her up. Scowling, I bent down and half dragged Thing One and my sorry-know-it-all-ass out of there. I didn't bother to say "bye" to Sally, or the much deserved, "You were *so* right, Bitch."

Later, whenever I'd teach *"Discipline and Control"* classes, I'd tell that story just to emphasize that although one might think that you don't have to "get burned to put out the fire," it surely does make a difference in your reality. Our best parenting is done by mistakes and humbly remembering that in the long run, the kid is going to teach you more than any course. And, it basically is about the Love.

The Love thing is intense. When they are under ten, they are so cute and let's face it, it's the last time your kids will actually go with you, when you want them to, without an argument. After that, you are simply a chauffeur to their busy wonderful lives. They are busy and you are driving, because you are convinced that your child is a potential Olympian swimmer, gifted dancer, will cure cancer, be accepted into Julliard, be a professional basketball star or a brutal hockey pro, soon-to-be-drafted into the local baseball team and so on.

We believed it. That's why we have virtually no discretionary income what-so-ever during our children's formative years. Every nickel, dime and seven-hundred-dollar check goes into soccer club membership, pre-swim meet dinner fests for thirty youngsters, ten pounds of oranges for healthy snacks, uniforms, personal coaching, not to mention tutoring so we can get them into a college that we cannot afford. Love and the insane belief that *our* child is *really, really* special, are the reasons we are still in the car picking up our kiddies from after-school enrichment art school, tennis clinics, school play rehearsals, in the dark of night.

It is the motivation to start dinner at four o'clock in the afternoon, so we can rush to practice to pick up our hungry offspring, and have a picture-perfect dinner awaiting the family. When we work full time, that dinner probably has been prepped at five o'clock in the *morning*, covered in plastic wrap, awaiting the hordes when we stumble home. What else but the Love could explain why we have spent every Tuesday afternoon, Thursday evening and Saturday mornings driving to some distant and wretched land?

As a parent/chauffer, you've already noted that all games, meets, tournaments and dance contests, begin at the crack of dawn. All tournaments are held in barren towns with names like, Last Chance, Sad Endings or Dead Man's Post. Most are located in the northern reaches of our most unattractive states: the upper east side of Wyoming, the far eastern line between Colorado and Kansas. You will not be going to any fun tournaments in San Francisco, trust me. Death Valley, you betcha.

Apparently, coaches, gymnastic instructors, karate masters, and others do not have a life on Friday evening and you shouldn't either. Nope, it's important that you and the kids each wolf down a high carbo dinner (that you lovingly prepare) and go right to bed by eight-thirty, so you can be up early to make a light protein-heavy breakfast, pack the car, five water bottles and the group snack along with your now-cold cup of coffee. You will need that energy to drive aimlessly to the pool, park, pier, gym or dojo by *seven* o'clock, Saturday morning.

This belief in the unique giftedness of our children starts at babyhood. What else explains why we spend the hundreds of dollars on baby-gymnastics for a seventh month old? It's a guilt ridden gut reaction to our conviction by some child development activist that our children would never walk normally unless we paid baby-gym lady two hundred dollars a month to professionally encourage our tot to roll. Hey, I have a Master's Degree in Child Development, and I can tell you that every child sans those with severe disabilities *ROLLS*. In fact, you got to keep your eye on them at all times or they'll roll right off the bed and out the damn door!

But never the less, we all do it: we are good parents and offer our children a plethora of opportunities to be, well, "just them." Only it is a soaring, extraordinarily gifted "them." Of course, this soaring and roaring down the highway in a carpool full of four-year-old hockey players can interfere with not only our personal self-esteem and worthiness, but more importantly, our other household chores. Hence, I created the portable laundry folding technique.

This concept flowered during practice time for whatever sport, dance, art class your darling might be taking; the teacher and/or coaches really do not want your expertise on the field "encouraging" aka, *nagging*, you potential Olympian/future, Picasso, Meryl Streep into performing better. You are supposed to disappear, and reappear exactly one second before practice ends. Now some moms go to the grocery store, meet for coffee, while other even bolder ones go get their nails done: but that can be dangerous. I mean what happens if you have to reach down and use those hands to release the trunk lever? You'd have to wait until you're at this end of town again before you could fix the nail.

To tell the truth, I prefer to read. It's a real treat, but while teaching part time, I found that I was mostly correcting papers.

That made me resentful. Actually, reading made me feel guilty. Surely, I could use these hours more productively? I must be neglecting something. Or it gave me a headache. Let's face it, reading in the fading light of dusk, illuminated by the weak excuse of an overhead light the size of your child's nightlight with your back plastered to the damp leather of an SUV seat that has only two adjustments: *forward* and *not so forward,* is not conducive to pleasant reading. If I put it into *recline*, well then, I just might fall asleep and lose my mother-of-the-year award because I'd sleep through the pick-up time. Mind you, said kid might only be six yards away, but all good parents are expected to remain *near* the field, gym, or wherever, eagerly waiting to greet their athlete, genius, and ballet prima donna, ready to swoop them home, out of the way of their trainers.

I had two girls both in sports, a carpool running for each, and each girl across town from the other. So, going home for quality/private time or house chores was out of the question. I was trapped in soccer/swim/gymnastics land, and as you know, these sites are never what I'd call "inspiring." You're either in a warehouse or an *abandoned* strip mall. Or in the middle of a rejected site for a federal prison—someplace that doesn't even have gas stations nearby. So, I maximized my time. I started hauling *two* laundry baskets around. I'd have the unfolded clothes in one, and the perfectly folded, stack neatly into the other. Upside down, the basket made a lovely workstation.

It was a good activity; it made me feel productive and kept me from running on to the field and beating up the practice refs. Hey, once I got a portable TV in the minivan I was set! Yes,

I admit it: I am so old that they didn't even have the high tech, TV play station in the vans yet.   Let me tell you, duct tape is amazing. I could strap down a mini TV right on to my console, added a couple of coat hanger extensions to the antennas and I was set: folding while watching Oprah. I had a little mindless fun (TV) and fine motor development (folding). Emotionally, I had a moment of feeling like things were in my control. Then a quick throw of an old bed sheet over the product to protect it from the five soccer bags and I was good to go.

Of course, the *games* were another story indeed. I was fiercely supportive of my children. I'd kidnap anyone foolish enough to be standing within four feet of me on my way out to a game, tournament, swim meet, race or match. This translated into the possibility that at any given time you'd see my husband or sometimes, the grandparents, who had foolishly made the mistake of "dropping by," hijacked into attendance. If a stray neighbor happened to wander on to the front lawn, well then, he was fair game to be hauled to the soccer field.

Once I even chased away a homeless guy who happened to be dismantling my trash bin when I threatened to take *his* sorry ass into the Suburban, forcing him to attend a six-year-olds' soccer game, if he did not cease and desist immediately. He ran, terrified.

Once there, I expected everyone to rivet their absolute attention on the Gifted One, aka Thing One or Thing Two. This focus is required in all aspects of your child's life and accomplishments. Hell, both of mine were in *college* and they still beam if I'd put their essays, grades and awards on the refrigerator. So, you watch the game with more interest than the polling places during an election.

I even read up on it so I become kind of expert, well sort of. I took a special interest in soccer. I wanted to be able to scream out not just epithets, but smart things like, "Off Sides!" or "Red card that fool!" These outbursts led my fellow parent-team mates to think that I actually *knew* something about soccer. So, when our coach, Mr. Sparks, had gallstones and no one else wanted to coach, guess who ended up guiding the careers of nine world champion, eight-year old soccer players? What a fool I made of myself. I'm surprised my kids and husband didn't enroll into therapy.

There I was, really into it, as they say. The other parents were so grateful that they were not going to have to stand in the field at 5:00 PM in howling rain and sleet that they bought me a team shirt. Of course, you realize that there are *no* sizes. All adult shirts come only in *Men's large, x-large and xxxxx-large.* So anyway, there I was, really done up in my bright school bus yellow shirt, lovely silky shorts that simply highlight the deep blue veins of my legs, those sturdy and so attractive knee socks, with the nifty yellow band around them and oh, let's not forget, instead of number on my back, I had that proud moniker of *Coach*.

I had my coordinating blue hat, sadly with my *first name* emblazoned on it, thoughtfully purchased by my husband. I attempted to pull down the hat in an effort to cover as much of my face as possible. On-lookers thought that I was trying to hide my cagey eyes from revealing my cutting-edge soccer strategies, but no, I was just trying to *hide*, period. My husband, who before my promotion to Coachette, was a normal, wrinkled T-shirt kind of guy. He then had secured his own matching stupid large person soccer uniform, that he has cleverly scripted with *Coach's Husband* on it.

I really knew that my reputation in the old neighborhood was shot. Instead "Hi M, how are you doing?" I was getting, "Hey Coach, way to go!" But really more often, it was, "Nice *effort*, Coach. Maybe next game." It was grotesque. I led that little team to six victories and eleven losses, and thank God, finally the parents gently, but firmly fired me, and hired someone who actually knew what a halfback did. What was neat is that my youngest child actually thought I was cool. Hmm, it is possibly the last time she ever thought that.

Now that I was not longer burdened with the awesome responsibility of being a coach, did I relax? Of course not. Traveling teams need chaperones.

We will discuss this chaperone position throughout this book as the job frequently crops up in the world of motherhood. When my eldest daughter was on the Varsity Team of her high school, I was of course *really* visualizing the World's Cup at that point because she was a junior and I just knew she'd have a Big Future. I volunteered to accompany the girls' team to Tempe, AZ for *The Big Tournament*. It was April. That is normally a spring month, but not in Arizona. It was hotter than Mars and full of dangerous aliens, i.e., *boys*.

These are not the normal, skinny, awkward, pimple-covered, geeky boys, but instead, athletic *male*s: sweaty, sexy, firm, horny. And those are just the soccer competitors. In addition, Tempe is a college town, full of young male college students. And here I was with fresh meat: twelve sixteen-year old girls. We stayed at some "No-Tell-No-Care hotel." You know it's cheap when you get the "breakfast" consisting of orange col- ored scrambled eggs, a flat English muffin and watery coffee for free. Most importantly, it has an overpriced, only-one-kind- of-red-wine-bar where one would find most of the mommies. Trust me, keeping teenage girls in line outside of a cage, will drive anyone to drink.

The bar was located in a spacious alcove, decorated with listless half-melted plastic philodendrons. I learned from the other more experienced mothers, aka, the *senior moms*, (this a reference to their child's position in high school, not their own premenopausal state) that one positioned oneself right on the torn faux leather coaches, near the foliage, directly across from the elevators. You did this so if you looked up, you could spot your darlings exiting their room.

The Great Exodus, is nothing more than a concerted effort by the nubile to get laid. This adventure usually happened about twenty minutes after you had visited the girls' rooms, cheerfully saying goodnight, "Good night girls, sleep well. Big game tomorrow!"

As soon as your back was turned and you were headed down the elevator, they were bee-lining it *up* to visit the Argentina boys' soccer team for some cultural exchange experience, or as I call it: *La Viva Loca*. Their goal and apparently, this repeats itself every year, so you'd think that someone would get smarter, was to take the ride up to the *seventh* floor and then take a secret elevator to floor twelve. It seems that the hotel housed the male teams from floor seven to "heaven." I really did take a moment to chuckle, remembering that I myself had assured a worried mom, that yes, the tournament was coed, but the girls played girls and those boys, well, no worries, they were on an entirely different floor and wing of the hotel. *Dummy.*

Now I understood why it was so hard to get volunteers to chaperone. I discovered that when you chaperone, you drink at the bar, and shout up occasionally, "Hey Shannon, back in your room right now!"

Or, you'd hear a mom rasping into her cell phone, similar to a Secret Service agent guarding the POTUS, "Sherry, are you in elevator bank C? Yes, okay, good, there's a potential unwed mother exiting floor eight via the *other* conveyance."

Sometimes it was a friendly shout-out, "Hey you, cute boy in red baggy pants, get your foot off our floor or I'll break my size nine shoe in your butt!" Naturally, you have to be able to say this in French, Spanish, Portuguese, Italian and German. You see, the goal of chaperoning is to make sure the girls are fed, rested, win the game and if possible, come back virgins. Oh, no, I'm being unrealistic; let's just make sure they all come back *not pregnant.*

Funny, I thought I'd get a break from the yelling, nagging and worrying and just have fun and maybe even sneak some shopping in. *I was so wrong.* By the following morning, I was pretty crabby. I basically didn't sleep all night worrying that someone was going to conceive an illegitimate baby under my watch. The girls however seem pretty chipper and in fact were ravenously hungry. No doubt their hunger stemmed from running up and down stairs, followed by their dashing and crouching into elevators. My charges started stuffing those funny looking eggs into their mouths. A few smarter ones, opted to pay some money and get safe things like, *Have a Diabetic Coma Belgium Waffle with Strawberry Jam, Maple Syrup and Two cups of Whipped Cream Breakfast.*

About an hour later, and two hours before the big final tournament, the Egg Eaters got diarrhea. This was followed by violent barfing, moaning and crying. The remainder of the team played and sadly, lost. I got to stay indoors with wadded tissue up my nose and mop up. The sickness went through the night and after three trips to the pharmacy for Lomitil, Rolaids and Pepto-Bismol, at three in the morning, it stopped.

By that time, I felt like *I* was going to throw up and wondered if one could catch food poisoning by osmosis? We boarded the plane like zombies and the first thing my husband said to me when we landed was, "Did you ever pick up my laundry before you left, because Mrs. Wang says it's gone." I was too wiped out to answer him or better yet, hit him.

The thing is, that we live to serve, and we serve so we can all live, and you know, it's really OK. It is after all, about The Love.

CHAPTER THREE

"Ah, Excuse Me Sir, Are Those Your Testicles?"

SOCCER HOLDS SO MANY MEMORIES. LET ME JUST SHARE a few more. Soccer practice occurred every Tuesday and Thursday after school, four to six in the evenings. As I said, half the time you live in the parking lot, or if you're allowed, the outskirts of the field. It is just easier. The games were usually on Saturday mornings promptly at eight. In the summer and early fall, it was swimming. From mid-September to November, it was soccer. Tournaments usually were during Spring break, which meant that you never took a vacation unless it was to the playing fields of Grand Junction, Colorado or the dry flat lands of middle California. Memorial Day was absently reserved for the Big Western Region games.

I do have several very special moments. Lest you think I'm going to start telling you about my daughter's fantastic goals/swim times/back flips or horse jumping skills, no worries. I might try to do that, but first I have to share with you a highlighted moment: *Mr. Testicles*. I was sitting in one of our lovely portable lawn chairs, which thirty years later, we still own. They will last forever as they are made of some kind of kryptonite that has a radioactive half-life of three hundred years. I'm sad to report that those chairs were sat on more than any furniture in our house. We schlepped them to every swim meet, soccer game, school picnic, and well, they probably would have gone to the girls' bat mitzvahs and graduations if my kids hadn't threatened to leave home. I like the chairs because now they sag to fit. One dips about three inches, cupping my sorry ass just perfectly, the other fits my husband's wide bottom, flat butt, as well.

So, I was sitting, idly leafing through a magazine before the game starts and this man, whom I assumed is the father of a girl, since this *is* girls' soccer, leaned down and asked, "Do you mind if I use your chair arm, I need to tie my shoe?"

"Sure," I replied politely. I continue to read my magazine, enjoying my illegal self-time.

"Yeah, these damn laces always come undone."

"Uh huh." I wondered why he thought that I gave a shit if he couldn't tie his shoes?

When his foot poked my arm, annoying the hell out me, I looked up, squinting at him. He was tall, pretty damn homely and wearing running shorts, track shoes and what should have alerted me, a "wife-beater" undershirt.

His shoe came down right along my arm. There was now grass on my arm. I shifted and looked up to tell him to move his foot off my sweatshirt and that's when I saw IT or should I say, THEM? He had apparently forgotten to wear his proper *support garment* and I was getting a doctor's view of some very hairy ugly "private parts."

I gasped and blurted, "Excuse me sir, but your testicles are falling out of your shorts!"

Now I have checked with my husband and other male friends and they assure me, that one's balls do not just "slip out" without one feeling it and I believe them. After all, if my boob suddenly oozed out of my bra, believe me, I'd notice. But this guy just *ignored me.* I mean there they were, dangling while he slowly tied, then, give me a break; *retied* his shoes!

Disgusted I leapt off the chair and in doing so ended up flat on my back and lucky me, right under his now elevated knee.

"For God sakes, man, cover yourself!" I yelped.

Moron squinted down at me and put on this fake-what-did-I-do-huh? face and has the nerve to look offended.

He snarled at me, "What the hell is your problem, never seen a set of balls? You prissy-ass housefrau." And then the asshole stomped off.

Prissy-ass-housefrau? I was left there with grass in my hair and the vision of dangling kiwis before my eyes. I heard the soft murmur of suppressed chuckles and saw two girlfriends hiding their grins behind painted acrylic fingernails.

"Oh, I see you've met Jason X," they cooed.

"I see you've all met him and *them* as well," I snapped back. The girls then told me that Mr. X was newly divorced and apparently had decided to take the "direct route" to find a sex partner. Like a peacock, he was known to go on full display at any given moment. It was surmised that Mr. X was *really* proud of his testicles and found all sorts of ways to share the wealth. I was assured that it could have been worse: apparently, he did a similar trick at the swim meet while he was less-than-ensconced in bikini shorts. I tried not to imagine how *that* might have looked.

"Well," I huffed, "if he does it again, I'm calling the police. That guy is a sex offender! Whose dad is he anyway?"

Disturbingly, no one could remember if he even *had* a kid. Thankfully none of us ever saw him again. Maybe I broke the bank. I dunno, but, *ugh.*

Then there is the time I took the kids' great grandma, aka "Lil' Gramsie," to the soccer game in Cheyenne, Wyoming. Now I know that the people of Cheyenne are lovely folks, but I am telling you that I have been there in summer, fall, spring and winter, and no matter when, there are always windstorms. If it's winter, well, then it's snow blowing—the kind of snow that leaves your face red and your nipples raw. In spring, flower petals, chased by pollen; in summer, the ass-kicking wind blows up so much gravel and sand, you feel like you're in Iraq.

We were going to a major soccer game and I picked up our the then, eighty-four-year-old great-grandma and positioned her into of our little folding designer chairs. I bundled her up in an ugly-but comfy plaid blanket, tied her wide-brim hat on her head, (she has maintained nearly wrinkle free skin, by avoiding the sun all her life).

Gramsie, ordered me to "go fetch me a coffee, Sugar, and bring me one of those doughnuts before they get all dried out. You know how I like my coffee, M?"

I nodded, "Yup, coffee, black. No sugar. Two napkins. Shake the doughnut so the sugar doesn't fall on you." I trotted over to the bad-tasting-over-priced-but-fund-raising coffee stand.

I halted, as the stand's tent was swaying precariously while the tray with doughnuts was teetering on a now *moving* card table. I joined another mom in an attempt to steady the bars holding the tarp, when I heard screaming.

A random mom was shouting, "Oh-my-god, the wind!"

I turned, and the doughnut stand collapsed and scattered across the grass. Little kids made a dash for flying sweets.

Then I heard, "Oh no, the outhouse!"

I looked over the field in time to watch the entire outhouse and its contents lift up, and like a failed blue rocket, land on my best friend's mini-van windshield. The outhouse was lying sideways against the parking lot, while its contents had apparently erupted all over the soccer field. Kids, parents, and dogs were running for the lives. The humans were holding their noses, gagging, while the dogs were making a bee line towards the foul pile-up.

I turned towards Lil'Gramsie, but she and the chair were gone! Seems the wind tipped her over and away she went, rolling down a knoll.

We found her, thank goodness, unbroken, but very pissed off. The aroma had triggered her bladder and she announced that she had to pee. There was nowhere to go, not that she'd ever be caught dead using an outhouse. I suggested that we continue over the hill and go behind the lone tree that had survived the prairie wind of Wyoming.

Gramsie replied with a scoff, "I am too damn ladylike to pee in the field like a friggin' cow!" Apparently, she was not too ladylike to swear like a friggin' sailor.

Kids were gathered up, seated on a blanket, while the two coaches conferred. I figured that this summit meeting would take a while, so I shoved Gramsie from behind into the van, as she never did get the concept of using the floorboard to step up into the truck. We drove through gush, slush and flying debris of unknown origin to the local burger joint with an unpronounceable name. Great grandma peed, and I got to hear her complain all the way back about the lack of toilet-seat covers, black fungus-covered hand soap, and the disgusting conditions of the restroom in general. I drove back, hopeful that the game would be cancelled, but no such luck. An unknown adult male with a large whistle and booming voice, directed us via megaphone, no less, that we were to pile into our trucks, station wagons, mini-vans and scurry around until we find another unsullied soccer field. Forty-five minutes later, we located one, thankfully protected from the wind by three scraggly trees. I think this one was in another state.

The worst was yet to come. We lost, 17 to nothing. After the game, I had to return to the Stinky Field and wait around for Auto Club to come and tow the port o'potty off my friend's truck. She was so shook up that I had to help her fill out the forms for the insurance company who'd never believe it anyway. It was just another day in the life of Love.

I didn't just express my love for my children by schlepping them around five continental states. I also made sure that every waking moment at home was an elevated learning experience. One day our cat, who was near-sighted and developmentally disabled, missed killing a bird, but did manage to have it escape out of her mouth and fall into the swimming pool. It was freezing ass cold that morning, but while my girls screamed pitifully, "Mommy, save the birdie," I dutifully waded into the pool and fished out the still fluttering baby bird. I prayed that the dumb thing would die a quick death, but no such luck. Thing One immediately got a tissue box and put the injured bird into a nice bed of $2.99 Extra Soft tissue.

Both girls then insisted that we make an emergency drive to the Wild Animal Center. There we were, bird and girls, in the back seat of my then Volvo station wagon. Me flooring the gas to get that bird to animal triage. As I drove, Thing Two gave me a running report.

"His wings are moving Mommy, drive faster!"

"Oh, he's pooping. He must be feeling better." *Don't we all poop in our pants as we die from a traumatic injury? I think being mouthed by a near-sighted cat and dropped in an ice bath constitutes a traumatic death... Isn't that why our mothers telling us to wear clean underwear in case of an accident is kind of stupid?*

"Mommy– his butt is bleeding. Drive faster!"

Then silence.

Thing Two sobbed, "He's not breathing!"

I exhaled, glancing at her through my rearview mirror, assessing how I can turn around and go home. I gently explained, "Well, it's hard for these little things to survive such trauma. He's really better off in heaven." I heave a sigh of relief. *Good, I can go get my nails done.*

"No Mommy, he's not dead. Thing One is giving mouth-to-beak-resuscitation." Mind you, this was before any of us ever heard of Bird Flu. I careened to the road's' edge and turned around. Yes indeed, Thing One had her once pristine eight-year old lips wrapped around the beak (a *bleeding* beak by the way) of the bird.

"Thing One–drop that bird! Take your mouth off that filthy thing this minute."

Thing One looked up, eyes glazed with accusation and tears, "But Moth-er, I'm trying to *save* him. "

"He's a dirty bird!" I screeched.

Thing Two burst into tears, and chanted, "Oh Mommy, I think you're so *mean. So mean.*"

Thing One tossed her head and rolled her eyes at me–a true precursor to my future with that child. "Well, he's *our* dirty bird now, so keep driving. *Please!*"

We arrived, delivered the now soggy-with-bird-blood tissue box into the arms of a zealous nut, who assured my kids that birdie would get the best of care. I know that kids think that when she turned around she was fluffing up the tissue. I secretly hoped that she smothered the thing. I figured that a brain-damaged birdbrain was not much of an option.

When we got home, the girls made me call every five minutes to check on Birdie's condition.

Meanwhile, I made Thing One wash her mouth out with Listerine twice. Then a third time for smart-mouthing me.

On my sixth call to the Animal Center, the attendant announced with a curt and annoyed voice, that *of course*, the bird had died. Both girls burst into tears. I made pancakes for lunch to distract them.

I was kind of proud of my kids. At least they had empathy for creatures. Since I had been a former science consultant for preschoolers, I thought *I* had a natural affinity for Nature. That can be the only explanation for why I willingly allowed animals so weird that the Discovery Channel could have been filming in our family room.

First, there is the case of the frog I brought home from the Science Discovery Store. We named him "Hector." Hector was a rare red-footed Amazon tree frog. He was damn cute. I guess, in looking back, he was a little big for a tree frog. He measured just over two inches–*that s*hould have been a heads' up for me. But hey, so he was a big guy, so what? It just meant that I had to make two stops to the pet store to buy filthy smelly crickets the size of wine corks to feed Hector.

The problem was, there was no filling this guy. He'd literally sit on his rock and chirp at me. I felt personally responsible for his meals as no one else seemed to care to feed our little science project. I'd cringe and throw in two to three crickets two times a day.

It was getting tedious. I suddenly got the bright idea that maybe Hector wasn't really hungry, just *lonely.* I know, I know, it was idiotic to give the amphibian human feelings, but *you* try looking at his weird little eyes and watch him hop around his aquarium paradise, only to face you no matter where you moved in the kitchen! I couldn't bring myself to make yet another visit to the pet store. I was however committed to Hector's happiness and was giving serious thought to finding him a playmate. One morning, when I was performing the morning ritual of rescuing dead mice from the pool filter, I scooped up a baby frog. He was cute as a button and of course, *young*. He spun his weird golden eyes at me and chirped. I translated that into, "Do I have a brother I could play with?"

I crooned at the green slimy thing, "What a darling little creature." Adorable. *And he will grow*. Hector can teach him how to eat crickets. I wondered if perhaps Hector would break off a head or leg and pass it over to the little fella. While I was contemplating the new family dynamics, I carefully cupped Little Guy in my palm. I called up to the girls to come see.

"I've got Hector a friend! Come see. Let's see how this tiny fellow adapts."

Thing One and Thing Two jammed down the stairs. Thing One warned, "Mom, I don't think that's such a good idea. The frog is really tiny."

"Nonsense. Frogs have little frogs all the time and–"

Thing Two chimed in, "But doesn't the mom lay her eggs away from the other frogs and doesn't the mom leave home too?"

Thing One shook her head and started to say something, but sick of their critical input, I basically blew my kids off and with a flourish, I threw in a sacrificial cricket and Little

Guy. Little Guy hopped around the tank. Hector hopped right behind him. Then the cricket attacked Little Guy. He managed to hop away–right into Hector's mouth. The girls started screaming. Hector, sadist that he was, was hopping around the tank with Little Guy's cute writhing legs protruding out of Hector's mouth. It was pretty gross and the girls were crying so loudly that a neighbor called to ask if I was using the Sally Method of Discipline on my children. Later that evening Hector was renamed Hannibal Lector. I couldn't look him in his revolving eye after that. One morning, I just set him free in the backyard. I hope some raccoon had a good meal.

Ah, raccoons. Another tale of Animal Channel gone badly. We had raccoons in the yard. I thought they were cute. In fact, I admit it, I used to leave cat food out so I could film their cute antics: eating, washing, and fighting. All of this was great entertainment. My husband admonished me, reminding me that they were dangerous animals and could be aggressive. I pooh-poohed him of course.

Until one night, I heard a banging on my office window. It was a raccoon demanding food. He'd bang, I'd look, shake my head, *not tonight buddy*; he'd snarl. I took issue, so I stopped leaving food. Ungrateful animal.

The raccoons disappeared—at least I thought so. One cold night, I opened the back door to let our dog out to pee. She charged past me and went wildly barking after what I thought was a cat.

"Bad dog! Don't scare the kitty. Come here, right now." The dog was going ape-shit in the bushes. I grabbed her tail. She turned, looked at me with crazy eyes and ran inside.

"Okay, that's a good dog, but come back and go potty."

Those were my last words, as a raccoon baby about the size of a house cat careened out of the bushes and attached it's claws to my arm. I was screaming. The raccoon was shrieking an unholy sound of frustration—probably wondering why-in-the-hell I'd stopped leaving cat food out, and why the hell was this *arm* in his way?

The dog, from the safety of the doorway (no Lassie rescue in sight for me), was barking and whining. The dog disappeared. She was smart; she was hiding.

"Help! Help!" I was trying to shake the snarling slobbering monster off my right arm, while crawling to the door. No husband. He couldn't hear me.

At last, the raccoon, thank God, got tired of me and ran off. Then I was lying in the hallway, blood everywhere. Dog finally found my husband. First thing out of his mouth was, "I told you not to feed them."

I grunt, "Fuck-you-get-me-a-sanitary-pad-to-stop-the-bleeding. I need a hospital."

He stared at his post-menopausal wife and asked, "Sanitary pads? We still have those? Where are they?"

I may have been in shock, but I could still be a bitch, "In the damn fridge! *Really.*"

He caught my sarcasm, told me I was meaner than a raccoon, and one more time, reminded me that I shouldn't have fed them. He finally brought back some pads that were in the first aid box. We drove in silence to the hospital.

Then he inquired, "Why didn't you just pull the thing off you?"

I mumbled something about a gun.

Upon our arrival, I was the most exciting thing the triage had seen in years: a raccoon victim! At least four medical personnel showed up to hear my story; some to share other horror stories they had heard, but until now, had thought were just "urban legends."

I was given a tetanus shot, antibiotics, along with five weeks of rabies shots, (thank goodness, they are no longer in the belly), plus twelve stitches. I have a wicked scar that is good for amusing, but somewhat icky, cocktail party conversations.

My now grown daughters think I should get a raccoon tattoo with a NO sign across the scars. I think a hummingbird would look better, but why tamper with such great conversation fodder?

Hector I spoke of, was one of many debacles attempts to have the unusual as a pet. We later had Juana the Iguana. When we purchased Juana, she was about six inches long. I was assured that she was a nice vegan kind of pet.

"Just fruits and vegetables—oh and a little cat food every now and then," the pet "consultant" assured me.

"Cat food? Doesn't that have protein in it, as in meat, flesh?" I queried, but the girl just patted me on the shoulder and helped me to my car with my $100 worth of tank, (we unfortunately had sold Hector's abode foolishly thinking we were done with the exotic pet nonsense), warming rock, gravel, mini-pond container, UV light, and fake trees. Oh, and special *iguana supplements*.

For one week, Juana *was* an interesting pet. We tried to

ignore that nasty habit she had of greeting everyone who walked by her cage with a hissing sound accompanied by the flaring of her neck rim. We just kept feeding her lettuce and bananas. Caretaking was no picnic. Iguana's toenails need to be trimmed. When one tries to do this–and it takes two people to do it, one has to hold the head away from any part of you you'd like to keep while your assistant attempts to handle a dinosaur size toe nail clipper. This activity goes on while a very long and gnarly tail is whipping around at you. Just picture trying to trim the toe nails of a small, but bad-attitude alligator.

And her cage smelled funky; kind of a combo of lizard pee-pee, poops that were larger than the cat's and rotted lettuce. It just wasn't fun, not any more, *at all*. Pretty soon no one was volunteering to do anything with Juana. Thing Two begged me to take the cage out of her room. Juana was giving her nightmares. The repetitive hissing and flaring actions were starting to freak her out.

I moved the lizard to the laundry room where she was doomed to have a boring view (no natural light), violent vibrating from the washer, accompanied by weird noises. Pretty soon, Juana was in a continual state of agitation: her neck collar up, her tail whipping about feverishly. I felt badly for the ugly thing. The lizard was dying of boredom.

So, it was kind of my idea to take Juana to Thing Two's fourth grade class for Show and Tell. I bought her in our cat's carrier, a cute little red lizard leash around her nasty scaly neck. Most of the girls squealed and the boys scrunched up their faces–no doubt to hide their terror. This pissed off Juana, so she started continuously flaring and hissing and thrashing her tail around. The boys loved that.

Thing Two spent ten minutes explaining the joys of owning a reptile with dead eyes and attitude. She walked around the circle and dared her classmates to pet the lizard. All the children looked at her like she was crazy and backed away. Juana responded by doing a big poop in the middle of the rug. That scattered the crowd fairly quickly.

At the end of the demo, the teacher came over and thanked me profusely for sharing the pet. She then added, "And I was so relieved. Last year, one of our parents brought in an iguana and it bit the tip of the mother's nose off right in front of the children!"

"But it's a vegetarian," I countered, eying our reptile with concern. Juana rolled an eye backwards, and flared at me. I swear her lipless mouth looked like she was saying, *"Fuck you bitch."*

I turned and threw a towel over my cold-blooded pet, tossed it into the cat carrier. The Cat never forgave me for that one and left. I drove, trying to ignore the thrashing sounds coming out of the cargo area of my van.

When we got home, I eyed Juana suspiciously. The iguana book said to let her roam around so she would adapt to her environment. I had a cat, so I was being a little reluctant to set the lizard free, but one day, I did.

All hell broke out. *Juana started chasing the cat.* The cat did not stand her ground. She acted as if she was being, well, *hunted.* It was at that moment that I noticed that Juana was no longer six inches long. She was now a foot and half. I also contemplated that maybe the reptile was hungry, *very* hungry. I quickly reviewed what I had fed her that day: two bananas and a cup of cat food. Just this morning, when I was distracted tiding up Thing Two's room, I'd forgotten to toss in an ugly brown banana. Juana had waddle up to the glass edge and started frantically hissing and flaring at me. I swear, she was saying, "Bitch, bring me my damn banana *now!*"

I walked down the hall to see Juana slithering/ sliding down our hardwood hallway, headed towards the cat. The cat was howling like, well, like a cat. Juana was hissing and slithering. I'd had it. I marched to the linen closet and got out a huge pool towel, threw it over the charging reptile, dumped it and the towel into a trash bag, and tied it into a knot.

The writhing bag and I drove to the pet store. The guy ended up paying *me.* Apparently, Juana was a "marvelous specimen." And, are you ready: *knocked up.* Yep, I had an unwedded lizard in the house. I didn't even want to think about how *that* had happened. Had the kids ever let her out at night to go cruising? I sighed in gratitude that I didn't have to witness the mini Juanas being born and then, most likely, eaten by their gnarly mother. In fact, I was so happy to get rid of her, that I refused to accept the guy's money. I didn't want to bring on bad karma.

As I drove into the garage, I was formulating my little lie to explain Juana's sudden disappearance; she'd gone to lizard heaven? She'd run off to be with her friends?

I thought it was pretty telling that absolutely no one in our family, ever *once*, asked, "Where did the iguana go?" I think everyone was just relieved that it hadn't eaten us in our sleep. The cat was never the same. I don't think she thought my actions were about love—at all.

CHAPTER FOUR

Parental Abuse and Foreign Relations or How I Invited the Sex Machine into My Home

WE SPEND THE FIRST SAY, FIFTEEN YEARS, OF OUR CHILDREN'S lives carting their butts to sports and cultural activities. Once they reach sixteen, your teenager starts lobbying to drive a car. We only had two cars, and since I was a stay-at-home-mom, I knew that my beloved van was the target of her aspirations. My eldest began what first was a barrage of nagging, begging and whining, to drive. Later, she cleverly changed her tactics. She would show up in the kitchen, seat herself on a bar chair, with a clip board note pad in her hand. She then would begin to read off reasons why *I*'d be gaining by her driving *my* vehicle. The most convincing one was that I'd no longer have to make dinner at seven thirty in the morning before manning the personal bus to carpool she, her friends, her younger sister and their accompanying entourages. The thought of being relieved of the hauling kids was enough temptation for me.

"But what if I need the car for my own doctor appointments? Or the nail salon, or hair, or--"

She rolled her eyes and exhaled, "Well, then, of course I'd let you have the car"

Whoa, she'd let me have my car? What-the-fuck?

Realistically, I'd have a back-up car as Husband often took pubic trans downtown. I caved in within five minutes. Let's face it, she had me at, "I'll even stop and run some errands for you after school each day." Of course, I told her that there would be no passengers for her until she'd been driving for at least six months, but I was all "yippee" for the errand running. Really, *how can we be so damn stupid?*

Within four months, she was already sneaking her buddies out to cruise, *forgetting* to pick up anything for me, and best of all, becoming pretty damn snotty whenever I'd remind her that she had promised to be my driving minion. Every time I'd reminded her to pick up bread or little sister, she'd moan that she had to go to soccer practice—*even though the season was over and it was snowing,)* or she had to stay late in the library. The library excuse really woke me up, my kid never stayed late in the library –ever.

It was a snowy day and I'd ordered her to bring the van back right after school, as I had numerous errands to run (remember those, the ones she was going to do every day?) and I had to take her younger sister to art class. My darling eldest groaned that she had "important things" to do and couldn't I just get someone else to cart Thing Two around and to run those errands? I kept my voice down and my fist uncurled, but trust me, it took monumental effort believe me. I heard myself actually *whining* to my own child that if someone didn't go to the grocery store soon, we'd be melting down the Tupperware and chewing on it. Finally, I resorted to the usual threats: car privileges would be over if…

She finally relented, acting as if I was threatening to take *her* car away, forcing her to pace at home like a caged animal every afternoon. Three o'clock came around, and no Thing One. By five, I was a combination of emotions that ranged from fear that she was dead to what I was going to plea once they found out *I'd* killed her. The phone rang at five minutes after the hour. It was her friend Lilly's mom. Lilly's mom sounded pissed.

"Are you aware that your daughter drove my daughter to school and had an accident and then had the nerve to just drop her off here not more than five minutes ago?"

"Nope, can't be. Because Thing One is not allowed to drive anybody and certainly if my darling Thing One had an accident she'd have called me up right quick." *Where was she? Where had she been? Oh God, was she doing something illegal?*

"Well, whatever you want to believe is fine with me. Just know that I do not want your child driving Lilly anywhere, ever again!"

She hung up in a huff and I just sat there in the kitchen huffing right back at the dial tone. Seconds later, Thing One walked into the house. I searched her face for signs of injury, repentance, and chagrin–anything that might reflect a violation and or a conscience. Zip. Nada. Nothing. I casually asked her how the library was doing; she mumbled something back and skulked towards the stairs.

"Hold it right there young lady!" I demanded, in my newly acquired authoritative voice

"Whhhhhhhhhhhat???" She rolled blue her eyes, that was the beginning of the first conscious onslaught of eye rolling behavior that lasted until she was twenty-five.

"Have you been driving Lilly around?"

Silence. Some glaring, as if I'm the culprit here. "Yeah, she needed a ride to school, so I helped her out."

"Thing One, are you lying to me?" *Wait a minute, why am I kind-of relieved? She already violated the rule of no-driving-friends!*

Silence again, which I construed as affirmation of low-down lying.

"And what's this about the van having an accident?"

I then causally walked towards our garage, determined to examine said vehicle myself.

"Mom, I really, really, really am so sorry about driving Lilly when you said not to. I promise I won't drive anyone else ever. Promise. And the van is fine. You go check it. No dents. It's fine."

She stood up and meandered behind me. I flipped on the light and examine the truck. It did look okay. "Her mom seemed to think that it was in an accident," I mumbled, confused.

Silence, which is always an indicator of something wrong, believe me. I mumbled an "all right, but this extends your pro- hibition driving others. It made no sense. There should have be an indignant argument going on here, not her compliance. That's how I figured out that something was *really* wrong.

"So, what *did* happen? Why did Lilly tell her mother that there was a catastrophe?"

"Mom, you know that her mother is the nervous type." She mumbled something else under her breath that I couldn't catch.

I felt the hairs on the back of my neck spring up. "Yes, and tell me what-in-the- hell happened?" I wasn't sure what was up, but I was relentless.

"Well, I drove over something."

Oh, dear Lord, what? A dog? An elk? Person? I waited. Thing One shuffled from one foot to the other, twirled her hair and rolled her eyes and exhaled, "Oh, it was *nothing*, just the median on the road, no big deal."

I shrugged and thought, *well yeah, that's not such a big deal.* Medians are about curb height and after all, the truck has four- wheel drive. But I caught her cautiously moving backwards out of the garage and flipping the light off. I squinted at her as she shrugged her shoulders, and gave me a wry smile. Sixteen year olds don't give you random smiles, wry or otherwise. I flipped the light back on *and* opened the garage door.

I walk around. Yep, no dents. Everything looks great. Except. . . except, the car is *tilting to one side*. A lot.

Turns out that Thing One did indeed drive over the median.

"But it was snowing and it was covered up Mom. It was just a *little* bump, really Mom. I wasn't even going that fast. It was *snowing…*"

It took more badgering and threats, plus an examination by my mechanic who shook his head, and determined that to have done so much damage, she had to have been driving at *least forty* miles an hour.

She tore out the drive shaft, train and two struts. The "incident" as she insisted on calling it, occurred on November 10, 1994. I didn't get the truck back from the shop until February 14, 1995. That was a hell of a Valentine's gift. A lotta love there, I tell you. I mean, I thought I was pretty damn commendable–not killing my kid and all. I just ran around hostile-passive-aggressive for five months. Not to mention my rental car was a Volkswagen Bug.

It was only a few months after I got back old "Big Green," as we use to call the truck, that Thing One announced that we were going to be "honored," (I swear, she said "honored") with, "a *wonderful opportunity.*" Again, these were my daughter's words or perhaps they were the delusional uttering of the crazed Foreign Exchange Student Coordinator. Apparently, there was a "young lady," Silia (who I affectionately now remember as *Silia-the-Unmanageable-Slut,*) who could not find a family to *sponsor* her. "Sponsoring" is a euphemism for "taking on such a horrendous responsibility that when it's over you want to have your head examined," but what did *I* know? I was just an innocent mother.

Within five minutes of meeting Silia, I understood why no one had accepted her. In fact, later, (much, much later,) I learned that our family was Silia's third attempt to find a host that, to use the Foreign Student Exchange Program's lingo, "fit" her "special needs." What that translated to was: find a family with enough gumption to try to wrangle a five foot five, 120 lbs., breast implants since she was twelve, spoiled and rich, fifteen-year-old.

Our charge arrived on our porch at 11:00 PM. Mind you, the Coordinator had assured me that Silia would be "right over," about five hours ago. I don't even want to *know* where she was until that moment. She was carrying a duffle bag–by Prada. She flashed me a charming smile, all teeth straight and white. Someone in a third world nation had forked over big bucks for perfect teeth, never mind the boobies. Silia from Paraguay was a delightful girl. But I knew that I'd have my work cut out for me. Just a duffle bag, and the kid was supposed to be staying with us for *six* weeks.

I stared at her in shock. She was wearing a micro mini, grommet-studded-thigh-high black patent boots, and a crop top. Her navel was pierced with what looked to be my anniversary diamond ring. Apparently, she did not own a bra. However, she did have an American Express Black Card. Undoubtedly; she'd be needing more luggage later. I couldn't help but stare at her nippley size C's–it was brisk here in Colorado. I worried over her five-foot-plus frame toppling forward.

She noted my rude stare, looked down, giggled and volunteered matter-of-factly "Maybe my new boobies are gonna need a sweater!" No mention of support garments mind you. I tilted my head in confusion. I'd heard that the Latin American parents were watchful and conservative. *Not.* At least, not when said ward is visiting the United States.

Almost immediately, Silia insisted on calling me "Mommy" which I thought was really sweet and *she* thought would be useful when she had to explain why she crawled out of our second story window to meet other South American exchange students for a little "fiesta" at 2:00 am. Apparently, my ignorance had forbidden me from understanding that she was just getting warmed up just when I expected her to be home for a curfew.

She had this cute endearing little thing she would do; start every sentence with "Mommy," which I liked because currently, my sixteen-year-old referred to me as, "Oh-my-God-Mother-How-Stupid." It was nice, I thought, to be called "Mommy" again. I can be so damn stupid, it is, well, stupefying.

So, on the fourth time that I leaned out the window to grab her by her ankles in an assist to ease her back into our guest room, and it is three-thirty in the morning, mind you, Silia explained to me; "*Mommy*, we no have a good time until around two–so you cannot ask me to come home so early. Twelve midnight is no good. Is no fun Mommy." Her bottom-possibly-silicone-injected-lip poked out, while her long black lashes batted at me sadly.

Interesting enough, Thing One didn't even try to pull this one off. Instead, she cowered under her covers in her room. I noticed though that she didn't "narc" on our visitor either, so I was well aware of who was in the enemy camp.

I looked down at Silia's muddy little Prada sneakers and I snarled, "Well I don't give a damn about cultural norms.

You have your exposed hinny back in the house by twelve midnight *on the dot* and there will be no more going out on school nights. I *mean* it, if you don't cooperate; I'm shipping you back to Paraguay." I folded my arms and felt like I had made real progress in managing teenagers. Logic never prevails—only threats.

"You can't! My parents are out of the country. I can't go home. There is no one there but Magdalena and she's a bad babysitter for me. She is our housekeeper and deaf!" She stomped her muddy-over-priced shoe onto my beige carpet.

I couldn't believe it. I was letting an uninvited guest in my own home bully me. I finally got guts. I told her she was grounded and that if she left the house without permission for any reason, I'd take her nasty boots, all of her Prada accessories and I'd hold the credit card hostage. It was weak, but what leveraged did I have? I could call the sponsor, but I'd heard that she already was housing three "rejects' who turned out to be possible young Columbian cartel trainees and rumor had it that she was being threatened to be thrown out of her own house.

Silia did not drive, and Thing One knew better than to risk her own driving privileges. *Great*, the sponsor had a potential drug lord, while we had a genuine terrorist. Silia also came with lots of money and she wasn't above using funds to bribe everyone into silence including me. One day after we'd had "words" about her once again attempting to sneak out, she showed up with a Louis Vuitton bag for her "*little Mommy*." I did not accept the bag. About two weeks later, I swear I saw that damn bag the arm of one of the cheerleaders–the girl who drove a BMW to school.

That girl's family would have been a perfect fit, after all, most of exchange the students seemed to have come from very wealthy families. Silia spent two days asking about why all of our "help" was on holiday. I pointed to Thing One, Thing Two and her, and said, "Don't need it, I've got teenage slaves." Silia did not laugh.

I ceased monitoring the windows. *What-ev-er.* It seemed that things had calmed down, or I was simply shutting down. Until one day, Thing One came home with Silia, sat down at the table and giggled, "I am in love with the most wonderful man." Now when you have teenage daughters, a "man' is any boy without zits, and whose jeans actually stay around his butt crack. So I wasn't sweating it at all.

She proceeded to tell me that since she was so bright, she'd been bumped up to the senior level trigonometry class. Before I could shout hallelujah in praise, she brought me down by announcing that this put her in a class with a gender make up of two girls (one being Vita Slesinger, a piano-legged professional Mean Girl and my daughter, Thing One) *and* nineteen senior class boys. My daughter maybe was learning Trig, but definitely learning a few tricks as well.

"And I am of course smarter than Mean Vita and most of the boys, but–"

"Well how nice for you darling," I interrupted her, and leaned forward enjoying my role as co-conspirator. "So, what about this boy, er, man, er, boy-man?"

Thing One rolled her eyes and then narrowed them menacingly and growled, "I know you think this is funny, but it is not. I think I could actually be falling *in love*. This is a real *man*. He is *EIGHTEEN*."

Now *that* got my attention. She was just barely past sixteen and had engaged the interest of a man-boy of eighteen? I immediately tried to review in my head the Colorado penal code for underage dating. *OK*, I thought, *calm down. He's still some snot-nose dumb-ass teenager.* I'd met most of the senior boys either when chaperoning the Mother-Son Dance, or serving up the hot dogs for the lacrosse tournaments, basketball and soccer matches.

I asked with faked casual coolness, "So which guy is it? One of the boys, err *men* from last weeks' game?"

"No, he doesn't do those sports."

Ah, thank God, a geek. As bright as Thing One was, she liked her boy-men built and into athletics. After all she was the center quarterback for girls Varsity soccer, and Varsity swim team and–

"*He's a foreign exchange student.* And he is on the *European* ski team. He is from Spain."

Remember the scene in the Hitchcock movie where Janet Leigh gets repeatedly stabbed by Anthony Perkins? And their playing that weird repetitive screeching tone over and over as the knife stabs the shower curtain and we assume, poor Janet Leigh? Well, that's what I heard. I looked over at Silia the Slut, who gave me an upturn tilt of her chin, narrowed eyes and then I swear, a "Fuck you Mommy" snide smile.

"*Oi Si,* I've seen him. *Es muy wappo.*" Her words dropped into a whisper. I just know she murmured something derogatory in Spanish. Then I swear the little sleaze *purred.*

If there is one thing I've learned *now* about parenting, is: *don't sweat the small stuff.* I'm sure you've heard this, but what does it actually mean? It is not, whether or not your child has made her bed or even if he crashed the car. No ladies, one starts sweating when one's daughter and you have the following conversation:

"Moth-er" (impatience in her voice, after all, I did not whip around at attention as soon as she blinked at me.) She then turned to Silia and asked her *in Spanish* something that made the girl shrug her shoulders and leave the room.

"Yes, dear?" I looked up. I don't have time to figure out when my daughter went from bumbling Spanish to fluent conspiracy Spanish. I see that Thing One has perched herself on the edge of my bed. I perk-up. *We're going to have a mother-daughter chat. It's something serious; she had actually banned Silia from the room.* Suddenly I was sweating behind my neck. I felt like *I* was in the principal's office. I looked across at her.

"Junés' sponsoring family has invited me over for dinner." She raised a brow.

"His name is 'June'" *That sounds soft, safe...*

"Pronounced *June-ay.* Really, Moth-er."

Having been corrected for my lack of cultural awareness, I nodded dumbly.

Now normally, when a child gets invited to one's home for dinner, it's a good thing. It's nice. It means that the parents might actually be able to complete a sentence during the meal (only if Thing Two goes along as a guest as well.) But *this* invite was problematic.

"Sounds great, let me check on something, honey."

"Like what? What's to 'check'. It's just dinner." Apparently, Thing One had a low volume for patience. She hissed, "I hope you're going to be reasonable about this" Which of course translates into: *I hope you're planning to give in without a fight as I'm going to make your life a living hell if you don't.* I may not speak Spanish, but was a genius at teenager.

I stood up and exited the room, attempting long cleansing useless breaths. I found my host-family guidebook, and started searching for *Juné's* hosting family. Yes, his name is spelled "June" but it's pronounced with an "A," as in *Jun-nay-too-old-for-my-precious-first-born.* His full name was *Juné Rubio Fernandez. Holy crap: he sounds like some damn soap opera star, or, damn it, like a ski star*

I noted that the young man was residing at one of the Varsity Basketball team's forward's house. I guessed there were no ski team players' homes available. *Did the school even have a ski team?* The hosting mom was already the mother of four of her own boys, *plus* Juné. That was four too many as far as I was concerned. I tried to recall what the host-mom looked like. I remembered the young men, ranging in age from fourteen to eighteen. That alone was a red flag. I visualized her life: all those toilet seats, perpetually with lids raised, all that smelly laundry. This poor woman had been shooting babies out of what must be a very saggy uterus, once a year. I didn't even do that to my dog.

Ah yes, I remembered–she *was* a haggard thing. I'd seen her once at the manicurist, attempting to find her finger nails so that they could be shaped into something other than stumps. The manicurist, from Viet Nam, just shook her head and moaned, "Oh no, no, Missy. You've got to grow some nail first; there's nothing here but the bed-for-the-nail. No nail! I give you a hot oil soak and take these white gloves. You put on the oil, the gloves EVERY NIGHT."

She had lifted her listless head from her chin and murmured, "Does this mean that I can't just rest here for a while?" Her head dropped back down and the manicurist shook her head in pity and began slathering on oil, lotion and some kind of Asian secret ointment, all the while shaking her head with concern. The mom, I think her name was Joanna, I simply thought of her as *Poor Soul,* had hands that looked like they'd grown calluses. No doubt this was the direct result of dropping the toilet lids sixty futile times a day.

I recalled that I actually had been over to the lady's house, but had not really met her. I'd knocked on the door. It had creaked open. Two half naked young men swirled by and shouted over their shoulders, "She's out there!"

Apparently, the poor woman had fallen asleep outside in the yard, a tall tonic glass dangling dangerously from her lobster hands. One of the "boys" halted down the hall long enough to explain that last night Mom had single-handedly hosted the Varsity soccer teams' spaghetti feed and she had just sat down to "recoup". I asked lamely if they were sure she was still alive, and the kid just shrugged his shoulders and exhaled, "What-ever." I didn't have the heart to wake her, but I advised one of the semi-naked males to maybe catch the glass slipping from her claws before it broke. He gave me a frown and walked away.

There were boys everywhere, but no sign of the dad. I knew there was an Impregnator there somewhere. The father-person coached the club basketball and soccer teams. The only time I'd seen him was at a distance, with a whistle in his mouth, arm outstretched, as he barked orders. I supposed that every year he got off the field just long enough to stick another male child into his poor wife.

So, based on my memories, I concluded that "dinner at the host's house" might be pretty loose and not likely very well supervised. Obviously, I couldn't possibly state any of that to my daughter–the idea of five males running about and stepping over an alcoholic-induced unconscious woman would undoubtedly have appealed to Thing One.

I went in search of the girls. Both Silia and Thing One were munching on popcorn, their eyes glued to the television screen.

"Well, did you finish your *investigation*?" Thing One turned and said what I could only assume was another snide remark in Spanish to Silia. I was really regretting this second language thing.

I took a breath and began, "He's so much older than you. And he isn't even into your sports and--" I halted myself, noting how lame I sounded.

"Oh, he *does* play basketball, just not club. That's why he's staying at Ralph's house. Besides, what does it matter? He's...

very smart. And he skies, and I want to go have dinner at his house." Now she became a six-year-old: mouth in a pout, almost tears in her eyes, with a plaintive expression she added, "What is the big deal, Moth-er?"

I took a breath and responded cautiously, "Well, Thing One, I imagine that the host mother really has her hands full with all of her sons and Jun–"

I was interrupted by, "It's not just Juné; both Brad and Bill each have a guest too, so I don't see why you have to be so very, very weird." I heard Silia sigh under her breath in agreement, "Ah sí, sí."

I felt my blood pressure rising. There was going to be a fucking *army* of young men at that house. And here I was, with *two* teenagers against me; there was a reason I had a five-year gap in my children. If I was feeling under siege, think what that poor mom was enduring with more than six males against one poor mom; it was never going to happen under *my* watch. I'd have to stop it just for the good of that poor mother. I *girded my loins* and put on my bright-I'm-such-a-cool-with it-Mom expression, "Honey, then she really could use a break, so let's have Juné over here?"

She didn't buy it.

"No! I want to go to his house." She'd morphed again, now into a horrible whiny little bitch. She leveled her eyes with mine and explained to her moronic mother, "He invited *me*, which I assume means that Mrs. Evan's knows too and–"

I decided that being a reasonable parent wasn't really worth the effort. So instead, grabbed her shoulders and hissed,

"You know, I may have been 'born yesterday,' but I sure-as-hell-wasn't born *blind*. The only thing that poor Mrs. Evans is aware of is her Lemon Drop martini. So, here's the thing, Thing One, if you want to see that boy for dinner tonight, it's at *this* house and that's final." Just for good measure, I shot a scathing glare at Silia, whom appeared oblivious to my ire.

"Ugh!" Thing One shrugged me off, looked at me as if I were absolutely insane, which of course, we know I was. Clearly, I was acting bi-polar. Then she actually stamped her foot. "You are the meanest mother in the world, not to mention you're–you're–defamatory! How can you say such things about Ralph's mom? Why are you so damn unreasonable?"

I did pause on that–mainly because I was trying to remember if "defamatory" was a real word. Then I explained, in my most reasonable voice, "I am not unreasonable, but I am a realist. There's no way those parents are going to be able to chaperone you and–"

I barely uttered those words and she proceeded to start bouncing around the room, alternating screaming and screeching at me, "Moth-errrr! *Please*, I am begging you! Why are you worried about chaperoning me? This isn't the eighteen hundreds! He's a student, not a sex offender. You're crazy." She added a deep sigh for emphasis, "You should *trust me*."

The words were dramatic, but I wasn't buying it. I kept seeing that image of Mrs. Evans passed out on the pool deck, her tattered fingernails, slippery with baby oil barely holding on to a Scotch or gin and tonic glass and I cringed. Plus, I've got to admit, I think I was still sore from the destroyed van incident.

Trust you? Fat chance.

I crossed my arms. I took a deep I-will-survive-being-the-mother-of-a-teenage-girl" breath, and I exhaled, "Thing One, *Señor-Gorgeous-Hot-and-Smart* is welcomed to dinner tonight. Take it or leave it. You've got three seconds. Either I go to Tony's meat market or I go defrost some burger, and we eat sloppy Joes, *as a family*, no guests. Your pick."

Silence.

"Now I'll cook anything you want--"

"*Any...thing...?*" Her voice dripped snidely.

I took a breath. "Yup. But, you've got to drop the sarcastic attitude, or I'll drop six cups of sea salt in the cooking pot." There—*I could fight fire with fire.*

She ignored my threat and lifted her eyebrows in challenge, "Even *Prime Rib?*" She knew how cheap I could be, and she was so right. At that moment, I visualized a six-foot plus basket-ball–skiing-athlete, my husband, who has no self-control when it comes to slabs of meat, and a fifteen-pound $12.89-a-pound prime rib roast.

"Yes, of course. How about I give you a list and while you're gone, I'll start a chocolate cake."

"*While I'm gone?* What does that mean?" She tilted her head. I could tell she was trying so hard not to smirk in triumph.

"It means that it is not snowing and I *trust* you to go ALONE to the market in poor old Big Green and bring it back chasse intact, along with the groceries and my debit card with money still in the account. Okay?"

Thing One nodded, that slow triumphant grin could no

longer be suppressed as it stretched across her $3600 perfectly aligned mouth, "Okay dokey. Cool. Only I think he'd like a Harvey Wallbanger cake instead of chocolate. After all, he's European."

My Harvey Wallbanger cakes were renowned–they also contained 99% grand marnier, triple sec, and were soaked in vodka. It wasn't going to happen–it was an *adult cake* and Thing One knew that damn well. "Don't push it, kiddo."

My daughter bounced off the couch, stared off into space as if weighing her options. Then suddenly she walked around, leaned down and wrapped her arms around my neck. "Totally cool, Mom. OK, give me the keys. Can I take Silia? *Pleaseeeeeeeeeeeee?*"

"Didn't I just say alone, not two seconds ago?"

She sighed dramatically. "O.K. but Silia is pretty bored. I think she was going to ask you if she could go over to the Foreign exchange students study club." I glanced at Silia, whose eyes slid from my scrutiny, then she turned, and one eyebrow went up.

Damn these girls, I snorted to myself, *like those drug dealers study*. I threw my hands up in the air, and relented.

"Fine," I quickly scribbled a list and handed her my ATM card, shuddering as I did so. "I want a receipt and nothing on that bill but what I asked for, do you understand?"

"Sure, Mom, of course." She grinned at me as she and her co-conspirator dashed upstairs. No doubt they had to put on their makeup before running a shopping errand. As soon as she left, I had the queasy feeling that I'd been played; that maybe she'd wanted to have the guy over here to start with. Ah well, we'd be eating well tonight. I guess you have to try not to sweat the big things either.

The rest of the afternoon was a blur. I was busy creating a feast-to-please in less than three hours. One shock: Silia and Thing One, with an additional bribe of wearing some coveted pierced ear rings from Thing Two, cleaned the entire entertainment level—except the kitchen which I shooed them out of. Later, Sly Silia, volunteered to make a salad. She was fascinated by raw greens, explaining that it was something rarely enjoyed in Paraguay.

I was really developing a bad attitude about that kid. Everything she said was suspect to me. What exactly did she mean by "greens"? Was that a marijuana reference? Was I crazy? Answer, of course I was nuts: I had two teenage girls in the house, not to mention the pre-teen lurking in the background.

My husband arrived home, and I decided that less information was the best information. With Love and Husbands, less knowledge is best; I told him that a "young person" from Thing One's trig class was coming over for dinner. Exhausted from a day at the office, he just absently nodded and trudged up the stairs, one hand dragging his brief case, the other I had cleverly wrapped around a glass of wine.

I was rushing around like a mad woman, sucking up wine out of a plastic tinted green beverage glass whenever the kids weren't in the room. I had taken the time to change into some cute jeans and an acceptable long sleeve t-shirt, brushed my hair and painted my lips a nice motherly pale pink. I didn't want my child to be totally ashamed of me. Only problem was that I kept breaking out into an athlete's sweat as I buzzed around the kitchen like Martha Stewart on crack. As I skillfully chopped vegetables and whipped up my own meat sauce, I glanced up at the clock. Damn, it was nearly six and Thing One invited Juné to be here at around six-thirty.

At precisely 5:59 p.m. the doorbell rang.

I took another swig of the wine and grated, "Shit, don't the Spaniards understand the concept of fashionably late?" I plopped myself down on the dining room chair and squinted at the dust bunnies that trimmed the seats. I shook my head, *come on, it's a kid. Who cares if nothing's ready yet or if the house is dusty? Calm down.*

The bell clanged again and I was about to do what I normally do when there is a knock or ring, start screeching for someone, anyone, even the dogs, to get the door. This time for some weird reason, everyone rushed to the door, including the damn dogs. I got there first, with my husband sliding in right behind me. I noticed he was breathing weirdly. Thing One, Silia and Thing Two flanked us. Out of the corner of my eye, I noted that both girls were wearing a *lot* of eye make-up. *Thing One hated makeup*. The dogs were at rapt attention at the threshold.

I opened the door with dramatic flair.

"*Oh-la!*" I exclaimed, thereby using up the very little Spanish I had. I grinned and then I stopped breathing. Behind me I heard my husband exhaled under his breath, "*Holy shit: are you fucking kidding me?*" Then, he laid a hand on my shoulder and hissed, "Did *you* do this to us?"

I ignored my hubby and Thing Two who chuckled and murmured lowly, "Wow, he is really HOT." At my feet, even my dogs, both female, started panting rapidly.

Standing at my door was what looked to be a genetic combination of Antonio Banderas, Brad Pitt and Matthew McConaughey rolled into one unbelievably gorgeous hunk of a *man*. *This*, dear Mommies, was no *boy*. This, my darlings was TROUBLE. And what went through my mind as this Gift-to-the-Western World stepped into my house? You will be shocked and disappointed in my parenting. All I could think of was the how lovely my grandchildren would be or better yet, the babies *I* could make. I'm thinking that this fantasy was only fueled by the fact that I was pre-post-menopausal at the time. Believe me, my therapist made a ton of money when I brought this up later.

Yes, disgusting, but hell, he was eighteen (as it turned out, he was actually nineteen,) but no matter. I wasn't thinking properly or clearly. Yes, shame on me, but at least I knew that I still had a semi-functional female body. I was definitely not thinking at all. My pheromones were doing great though, thank you.

The woman in me couldn't help but to be proud that my darling little first born had snagged the interest of this yummy morsel. Sure, he was probably a pervert and wanted to get into her pants, but I didn't worry. I knew that the only panties that might actually slip off around here could be Silia's, and I actually was coming to realize that Silia was all talk, no action. Besides, Juné, showed absolutely no interest in her. Of course not, he wanted a blonde virgin to conquer.

I took a breath, remembered my manners and welcomed

the wolf inside our home. He brought flowers for Thing One, candy for me, a bottle of Spanish wine for my husband, *and*, a cute barrette for Thing Two. This kid was good, very, very good. We were doomed.

By the time, we sat down together (Thing Two felt the sudden need to change her clothes two times and Silia's micro-mini became a nano-mini,) the prime rib was pretty much well-done, but my husband was so thrilled to have a slab of meat on the table, there were no complaints. We ate dinner quietly, until *I* opened my big mouth.

"So, Juné, what are your plans after you graduate?"

He leveled emerald green eyes to mine and I swear, in a deep gravely-how-could-this-guy-possibly-be-only-nineteen-voice, replied, "Well. . ."

I want to add that these eclipses are here because that is exactly how he spoke, with long poignant pauses between each word; "I was hoping to find a..." (*pause*) "family..." (eye lash blinking, heavy pause), "to live with..." (pause) "while I attend the University here."

A family to live with. A family to live with. A family of lambs. A wolf in the barnyard. Nope, I. Do. Not. Think. So. I masked my nervousness with a really silly-putty grin. I discreetly, OK, *not* so discreetly, I admit it, eyeballed him. He was genetically perfect and I was sure, wealthy. I'd figured the wealthy part out when he indicated that his parents were divorced, (bad trait), that his mother living in Switzerland, (good trait), his father part time in Spain, other times in Italy (good trait.) I took a deep breath and offered the kid more mashed potatoes.

I spent the remainder of dinner attempting to steer the conversation away from Juné's future living arrangements. That was easier than ignoring the shotgun loading gestures my husband kept making behind the kid.

Dinner over, I sent the children downstairs to the home theater to watch a movie. I figured that my husband's home office was adjacent to the room, so he could casually chaperon and besides, Thing One would be accompanied by her pesky little sister and the bubbly Silia. Just before Silia jammed downstairs, I grabbed her hairy little skinny arms and hissed, "Silia, listen to *Mommy!*"

"*Sí?*" She drew out that last sound with a sly lift of her eyebrow.

Jeez, I had to stop hating that girl. "Silia, do not, I repeat, do *not* leave Thing One alone in the room with Juné! *Sabe?*"

Silia feigned helpful conspiratorial eagerness, "Oh, *sí*, of course Mommy. You no wana un *pequeño* Spaniard, *nino!* Heh, heh."

I used deep breathing techniques not to grab her and start shaking. "Yep, you've got it–no baby Spaniards. So, *do not leave them alone*–even if Thing Two is there, got it?"

"Okey-dokey Mommy!" Silia waved her hand and dashed down stairs.

Okey-dokey?

No more than fifteen minutes later, Thing Two had dashed up the stairs. "Mom, you better—-"

She was interrupted by Thing One who nearly crashed into her. I noted that her pony tail was undone. Her cheeks were flushed. She was struggling to articulate. That's okay, she did not have to say a word. I got it. My daughter had been compromised. All right, not exactly *compromised*, but disheveled, that's for sure. I was strangely calm. Then another, weird feeling went creeping slowly into my gut.

"Thing One, what happened?" I tried to ignore the "whooping sounds" emitting from Thing Two's mouth. *Where the hell was her father? I told him to Watch. The. Kids.*

Thing One breathlessly described to me that Juné Hubba Hubba Fernandez first held her hand, then within two Spanish minutes, started kissing her hand, specifically each of her fingers. This part was punctuated with my second daughter making big sloppy kissing sounds.

"And he used his tongue!"

"Oimigod! Where?" In her mouth? Or was it somewhere else that would force me to find that damn shotgun? *Do we even own a shot gun? How long is the wait period in Colorado?*

"I just told you—on my fingers. Moth-er–he sucked on my fingers and then--"

"Eww! Gross!" Thing Two put *her* finger into her mouth, and made an exaggerated a gagging gesture.

I held my hand up to stop both of them, and then in my most interrogating tone, asked my eldest, "Did he touch you anywhere else but your fingers?" I leaned down and gave her the old eyeball to eyeball stare.

"Eeww! N-no.... No, Mom!" Thankfully, she looked horrified.

I wondered how my dumb-bunny husband had missed all this; seeing as how his office is right next to the theater. Best that he had not seen it, he might have blown an artery. "And where was Silia?"

"Oh, well, she didn't want you to get angry, but the phone rang down stairs and it was her parents" Thing Two rolled her eyes in a frighteningly good imitation of her older sister, took a breath and dramatically exhaled, "and you know how hard it is to get through long distance from Paraguay? She just went to talk to them, but then she got disconnected."

Now, you have to see the insanity in this. The phone that was downstairs, in fact, it was in my *husband's office*. So that meant he had been completely oblivious to anything going on. I sighed tiredly and cautiously inquired, "And where is she now? Please don't tell me that *she's* with Juné!" I was already imagining us loading Silia's things on to the gangplank, her waddling behind us, big with child. I don't know why I was so hard on Silia, or on Juné. I knew I was acting like he was a gigantic foreign penis looking for a home. It wasn't fair, but I was a tad crazed.

Thing One, whose face was bright red and was deep breathing, explained, "She called them back. She's still talking."

I took a deep breath. I was being unreasonable. The good thing was that she wasn't dry-humping Juné. The bad thing was I was going to have a five-hundred-dollar long-distance bill.

"Where exactly is *Jun*é?"

Thing Two gestures down the stairs, "Oh, he's chilling on the couch, watching the Ecuador soccer games."

I looked over the scene. There was Thing One, panting, flushed, mussed-up. The culprit was sprawling on my coach, watching my TV. Then I did what any self-respecting mother would do when a gorgeous foreign exchange student has taken a pass at her precious daughter. *I sent her back down stairs*.

First I sprayed her with some perfume. Why, do you ask? It's very simple. I knew that they weren't going to, well, *go all the way*. Thing One would simply kick him in his shins. And, well, ladies, spank me, but when would a girl get a chance to make out with a god?

As it turned out, he did take her out on one date. She was back on the porch one hour and twenty minutes before her curfew. When I asked why, she fanned her face and said dead seriously, "Mom, he is just too hard to say 'No' to, so I told him no more dates!"

It was a treasured moment in parenting. My daughter's morals had prevailed, even if my own had gone slightly off-kilter.

Ironically, two years later, she was allowed to accompany my husband on a business trip aboard a corporate jet for one of his meetings in Telluride, Colorado. She was ambling down the through the famous ski resort, and whom should she see, but Juné, accompanied by his parents and no joke, an *entourage* of body guards. I had been right; he was a wealthy little bugger, and his father, it turns out was governor of a province. She told me that when she first spied him, she literally started to hyperventilate. But then she took a deep breath and, "You'd be proud of *me* Mom. I wasn't tongue-tied at all. In fact, I started speaking Spanish to his mom.

"But Mom, the best part was when I lifted my arm, checked my watch and said, 'Oh sorry, got to go and catch my dad's jet! See you sometime!'"

Silia, once she returned *intact*, to Paraguay, totally blew off Thing One. However, she wrote to her "American Mommy" for *three* years. Then she entered a nunnery. I don't know if she went willingly, or was the victim of family intervention.

After seeing each other in Telluride, Thing One and Juné became pen pals for a few months. Then he went off to Oxford, and she, to the University of Chicago. Thing One hasn't heard from him for years, but a few days ago she did tell me that kissing him was absolutely, well, awesome.

As it turned out, my slightly twisted view of Young Love, kind of paid off. I figure that years from now, when her widened rear-end is bumping against her aging husband's, she'll happily recall that hottie Spanish specimen. God knows I do.

CHAPTER FIVE

Follow that Purse!

SOMETIMES THE LOVE THING JUST STARTS TO MAKE YOU into a bitter woman. I mean all day long, you're thinking of others, your cooking for others and of course, you're spending for others. Sometimes, every now and then, a mother has got to crack.

I was reading one of *four* of my fashion magazines, gifts from my daughter, Thing Two, then nearly eighteen, and a real pain-in-the-ass. She said that the magazines were a remedial attempt to reform me. Once, long, long ago, when I was a size two, naturally beautiful due to being a mere twenty-five, I only read *one* fashion magazine. Of course, I could only afford one, but no doubt, I felt confident that I only needed a little bit of guidance, not a *library* of reference. Now, to avoid being Grossly Out-of-the-Loop, I have four guides to better dressing, eating, exercising, choosing and applying of make-up and yes, even self-pleasure. I'm not exactly sure why a good orgasm is relative to beauty. I think it has something to do with clear skin.

There is an external factor that contributes to this need-to-read. I am deeply entrenched in an ever-continuing battle to dispel the *Boring Mother Image* that has plagued me since my daughter turned sixteen. She diagnosed me and dutifully reminds me that I am indeed in danger of becoming a *Boring Person*. She added that it's one step away from being a bone fide *Boring Mother*. It does not matter that I am a successful college instructor, a writer and admired amongst my peers for my slim figure, energetic attitude and dedicated volunteerism. Nor do I get credit for that fact that through guile and hypnosis, I have managed to keep the same man, AKA, my husband interested in me for over forty years.

According to my Thing Two who fashions herself as a guru of style and who just happens to wear pants that barely cover her pubic, now public, area. I needed to "get with it." *Getting with it* excludes wearing jeans that I have owned since 1969. One afternoon my daughter was standing in the kitchen, supervising me as usual when she suddenly and quite violently did her hair flip thing, which of course, was immediately followed by the obligatorily rapid series of eye rolls.

Now those of you who have teenage daughters in the house will understand immediately what hair flipping-eye rolling communicates: *impatience, embarrassment, disdain.* She followed the flipping by an extended and painful sigh full of pity, and as I expected, exasperation.

"Mom, *why* are you still wearing the same jeans you got during the *sixties* for crying-out-loud?" Her question was followed by a deep, pained hiss.

Now, I would have thought that if someone can actually still *fit* into her jeans from over forty years ago, that one's child would be proud, or at least admiring, but apparently not. Of course, I realize that they "fit" because they have lost the will to live and the fabric now hangs listlessly on any shape or size. I made a feeble attempt at a defense, "Aren't they kind of vintage or retro?"

This smart-alecky remark was met with a scoffing look of disbelief, followed by the Hair Toss-Eye Twitch (again). I immediately realized my mistake. After all, I was on the receiving end of getting *two* hair tosses in less than five minutes. That had to be some kind of record for being out-of-the-loop, I am sure.

"*Moth-er*, as if you 'd know what vintage is. Come on!" She shook head in frustration.

"Child, need I remind you that I have a Master's degree and five credentials--"

I'm interrupted by a huge sigh and a quick snap-of-a-hair toss. *Again.*

I cringe, remembering when she once called me "mommy" in an adoring voice. Now a bright pink nail that I paid for is wagging at me. "Moth-er I don't want to discuss what *your* version of 'vintage' is, I just want to point out that those," she waved the nail up and down the length of my leg, "are *tapered.*

That's bad." She exhaled and shook her head, clearly forgetting how patient I was when I was teaching her how to shave her legs. I never once tossed my gray hair or rolled my eyes. I just calmly brought her the antibacterial ointment for her nicks.

She gets my attention, by impatiently tapping her feet. "*Moth-er*," (She likes to repeat this in two syllables.) She noted my chagrined look on my face, so she continued, gently chiding me, "I love you, Mommy, but really, *nothing* you own is 'retro,' just dated. GET. WITH. IT. *Please*."

I was stunned. I'm dated. I'm old. I'm out-of-it, and apparently so out-of-it, I didn't even *know* I was out-of-it. But on the bright side, she did say "please."

The next day, she bought me three fashion magazines and told me that in the evening, we'd be having some mother-daughter "face time" to review what I had "learned." I'll tell you, I haven't felt so much pressure since I studied for the GRE.

I was dutifully studying. Well at least thumbing through, but I admit it's difficult. First, there are so few people that I can relate to in most of these magazines. It appears that they have murdered any female who might be over the age of thirty and since I am well past that mark, I take it personally. As I idly slough through pages, I stop, enthralled by page one of a ten-page ad for Donna Karan. I turned the pages slowly, mesmerized. The tone of the layout was provocative and so erotic that I stopped and called my mother for permission to continue looking at it.

She told me to "get with it!" which reminded me that my daughter has inherited *her* genes, not mine. I tried to discuss this further with her, but she hung up because she had an appointment with her personal shopper.

I went back to the ad. The set and background made me think of somewhere in Asia. The first page showed us the back of a woman passing in a triangular straw hat. The woman's jacket was wrinkled. I immediately related; *my* clothes were usually wrinkled. Apparently, lovely tall brunette models are allowed a wrinkle allowance. *Hey, I've actually worn a similar straw hat! Wow, I'm starting to like this fashion stuff.* I did briefly contemplate whether or not the model carried a mini iron everywhere. Then I remembered that she has a battalion of dressers to fluff and/or flatten her clothes as needed. As I turned the page, a new even-more svelte model was wearing a bone white linen suit. The skirt skimmed her perfect-no-cellulite-no spider veins-thighs. There were a few strategically placed wrinkle-lines on the skirt emphasizing her never-had-a-child-boy-shaped hips. I say they were strategic because, they looked like they were ironed in on purpose, not mushed up as real wrinkles are. The sultry model was wearing nothing under that first-button-of-her–naval jacket. My suits do fit in a similar fashion: too tight.

However, that tight looked good, damn good, *and sexy.* Something right there caught my eye: slouched between her breasts was a leather strap of a slender yet formidable black bag. I noticed immediately that the strap was kind of squashing the girl's perky breasts. Since I have breasts that are yeasty, not perky, I felt that squashing was not an issue for me. Mine are easily retractable. In fact, they have been known to slide from center to side for no apparent reason other than boredom.

At first, I just stared at the bag and then I heard a whiny voice, "Some people get to have slender thighs, skinny waists and cool black bags like that." Bags that just kind of slouch onto one's hipless body. That was *me* whining. I leaned forward and studied the bag.

Then, it happened.

I sat up and I roared, "I-WANT-THAT-BAG!" I was obsessed: I had to have that bag.

It had to be subliminal. At that moment, I surmised that the ad must have had tiny microscopic writing that demanded that I buy the purse. I briefly remembered that Thing Two had a huge orthodontic bill coming up. Briefly. I turned the page as I mused, *why do I want that bag? It's silly.* I stared into the print ad, hoping my answers laid somewhere in the marketing strategy of Donna Karan NYC. Then it hit me: the *why.* The power of the bag: Jeremy Irons, the actor was hunched forward, his dark eyes had been intensely peering right at me over his wire rims—the whole time! How had I missed this? How had I not noticed that his lightly muscled arm was draped on the model's non-shoulder-bag-shoulder, his lips were brushing her neck?

I stared into the pages. On the opposite page, Jeremy was looking directly at the reader, (that would be me,) with his five o'clock shadow, those penetrating eyes that seemed to be asking me, "If not the linen suit, if not skinny thighs and perky boobs, then why not the bag? Surely even *your* body can support the bag." I imagined that he took a long damaging inhalation of his cigarette. "Well?"

I hesitated, embarrassed, trying to decide if I should answer him. I quickly had looked around the room for witnesses and flipped the page. I hated leaving that great close up shot of the little hairs on his arm, cleverly exposed by the rolled-up sleeves of his Donna Karan-for-men-shirt. When I turned the page, I saw *that* woman again. This time she was draped in a silk handkerchief creation full of little geometric shapes. The dress was pretty much see-through. It skimmed her shape like a sexy muumuu. I think I saw a similar dress on Rene Russo in the Thomas Crown Affair. *She* ended up having great sex on the stairway with Pierce Bronson. Briefly, I stepped up my fantasy. I could lure Jeremy Irons *and* Pierce Bronson? Cool. *Stairs might hurt though...*

The model was reclining on a pile of rugs, an old bicycle behind her. I just *knew* that she rode that bike to the little room while wearing that skin-tight white linen suit and *then* she changed into this flimsy thing. *That tramp.* Moreover, just whom was she expecting to meet here in the bicycle barn? Why was she slouched like that? Why couldn't *I* learn to slouch? Was that really different from *hunching*? Seems to me I'd spent many years telling Thing One and Thing Two not to slouch. Had I been giving them poor guidance? Was I a posture hypocrite?

I turned to the next page, and saw that my nemesis has changed clothes *again*. Well, that explained the wrinkly clothes; in this fantasy world one just crumbles up what I'm guessing was a $2500 linen suit, and pops on another fabulous confection. This time, draped over her non-hunching shoulders, was a pinstriped jacket, accented with a frothy shawl. The jacket looked like the current trend, "men's wear." Only then I saw that indeed it really *was* men's wear. *She had on my Jeremy's jacket.*

That sneaky bitch. The "shawl" was not a shawl, but another gossamer dress of some kind that did not keep her skinny butt warm. Therefore, she has stolen my man's jacket. This explained why he was in shirtsleeves in the previous picture. Meanwhile, the model had the nerve to stare back at me forlornly as if to say, "Do you think he'll want this back soon?"

I turned the page. Jeremy, the man who would soon replace my husband, apparently had taken *her* jacket. At least it fitted him: tight, barely containing his unbuttoned black shirt that exposed his great looking chest and a reasonable sprinkling of chest hairs. He looked disheveled, dark and very sexy. At that moment, I thought of our foreign friend from Spain, Juné. *Bad boy, very, very, bad boy. No, grown-up bad man.*

Jeremy's hair was shaggy; his face, worn, shadowed, sexy. I thought: *I want him.* I realized that this is a lapse of judgment and a sad fantasy. I am married to a neat tidy blonde sort of fellow. I had caught the flu for mussed, five o'clock shadowed men. Those hormones were sadly askew again.

I shook my head and dropped the magazine. I took hold of what I thought was reality and exhaled, "No, what I *really* want is that bag." Grown up me started to argue but my meddled brain retorted, *get the bag, maybe even get Jeremy. Well, okay, at least have a more interesting, fashionable life.*

Get a grip was also was echoing in my consumer's mind.

I opened the magazine and like bad marketing karma, the

page opened back to where I left off.

Jeremy hissed at me, "Stop being a Boring Mom Person and get the damn bag! What a ninny." This comment was accompanied by another imaginary exhale of smoke.

I am not a stupid person. I am not an impulsive buyer. I am a critical thinker, not a fashion slave. I resolved to retain my sanity and dignity, I turned the page, still compelled to at least "finish out" the ad campaign. I noted that my Jeremy was heavily making out with that stupid woman while luxuriating on what was probably, Donna Karan sheets and bedding. However, Jeremy was not looking at her, but rather at *me*.

Ah ha, I knew *exactly* what he was asking: *"Darling,"* (British accent here) *"Did you get the bag?"*

"Of course, not Jeremy don't be a silly. I am not a fashion slave or a Pavlov dog responding to an incredibly sexy ad campaign. I am a Boring Mother of two teenage girls, dear boy."

I quickly turned the page. He was looking down at the ungrateful witch's hand while she was pushing him away with the other pale limb. What a fool she was. I didn't even notice what she was wearing, but I did see *my* purse lying on the floor at her feet. I scowled. That was no way to treat such a beautiful piece of leather.

On the next page, Jeremy had maneuvered her to a mirror. They were gazing heavily at each other's reflection. Jeremy looked frustrated, yet I say, *horny*. (I hear this word a lot amongst my daughter's friends.)

I closed the magazine and attempted get back to my real life. I went to the counter. I peeled some onions until tears welled in my eyes. I diced some peppers into minuscule lumps. However, the image of that bag and adventures that one has in carrying such a purse, haunted me.

Finally, I could stand it no more. I rushed back to the table and I quickly opened the magazine and rapidly flipped past the other erotic provocative pictures of the life I would never have and wouldn't know what to do with if I did. Sure enough, on the last layout was a 1-800 number. I dialed it and damn it; someone actually answered the phone at 8:00 p.m. EST time.

"Hello, Marge speaking for Donna Karan Creations," a clearly New Jersey accent let me know that I had met my doom.

After hesitating a long time, I sputtered, "Hel-lo?" I was hoping that she would recognize that an idiot has called her and hang up.

No such luck. "Helloooooo? This is Donna Karan creations, NYC and I'm Marge and I'm here to *help* you." She sounded so nice, so. . . helpful.

"No one can help me," I mumbled to myself, "I'm screwed." I sighed, holding the phone a good ten inches from my weak chin.

"Beg your pardon, honey? This is Marge at Manhattan. Can'a help you, sweetie?"

I smiled at the New Jersey accent. Like a prisoner under torture, I coughed up my story. I described the ad in more detail than I'm sure Marge wanted to ever hear, especially with my sick spin on it.

"Uh-huh," she hesitated. I imagined her jotting down along the margins of her order pad; "*Crazy Person called 8:15 PM. Wants *to stalk Jeremy Irons—while naked holding a large black purse."*

But instead, a kind empathetic voice inquired, "So, sweetie, do ya want tha' bag or wha'" I visualized Marge shaking her head and chuckling as she planned on what she was going to do with her commission from this sale.

"Well, like–" Oh God, had I just erupted with *"like"* the way my kid says it—using it to punctuate every breathless hesitation in conversation?

I took what I hoped was a deep, calming breath and tried to sound fifty plus years. "So, you couldn't possibly actually have that purse, now could you?" It took maximum effort not to sound too pathetic or well, *hopeful.*

"Actually sweetie, we don't, but I can sure find out about it for you."

This was my out, but did I take it, oh no, I did not. Marge recognized that my pregnant pause was the salesperson's loophole and she went in for the kill.

"If you want me to, I can look. I'm not even sure that it's one of our bags. I mean it could just be a prop—or," now was the kill move, "one-of-a-kind."

"Oh, it would be rare?" *Yeah, exclusive, unattainable, like your bank account, fool.* I breathlessly asked, immeasurably relieved. *I wouldn't be able to get the bag because it does not really exist. None of it does. Not Jeremy or that wretched model or Asia, or any of it. Thank goodness.* My mind rambled on and I almost didn't hear Marge's next words.

"Ya know, if tha' bag is anywhere, *I* will find it for you, Sweetie, trust me."

Oh great. "Oh, okay." My voice sounded exactly as if I were four years' old. Pathetic.

Marge took my phone number and I hung up, exhausted. "Whew, close call. I almost bought a purse that I don't need or even know the cost. Thank goodness, it wasn't there."

All was well for about a week. I continued to read the magazines, carefully avoiding any sexy, appealing or cajoling ads at all costs. I put out of my mind, thoughts of exotic Asian vacations, me swathed in semi-wrinkled linen and my carrying a Big Important Black Purse, with Jeremy toddling behind, lathered in a passionate sexually frustrated sweat.

I was a Friday morning, specifically seven in the morning Pacific Standard Time, exactly eight days from my disturbing phone conversation with my New York City friend, Marge-the-Relentless-Saleswoman. I was sneaking in a cup of coffee before the end-of-the-week-whirlwind begins. I was calculating how many unfashionable hideous sweat suits I had to wash.

The phone rang. It was my *personal shopper*, Marge.

"Honey." That's how she said it; as if the salutation, "honey" was a sentence structure unto itself. I noticed that I've either been demoted or elevated from "Sweetie" to "Honey."

"Honey, I've got *really good* news for you."

"Oh yeah?" I suddenly developed a Brooklyn accent. *Good news*.

Marge, with breathless enthusiasm, barked, "I really checked out all our stores and guess what?"

"Wha?" My heart started hammering. I was walking slowly towards my office desk. I fumbled in the drawer, to retrieve checkbook. I stared blindly at the poor empty thing.

"We have your bag."

I frowned at my balance and stuck my hand on top of the bill pile instead. My eyes scanned over the Visa bill. *Not too bad...*

"Oh. You have *my bag*." I started sweating. *Shit.*

Now as soon as she said, "We have your bag," the damn thing *became my bag.* I mean I don't know how else to explain it, but all of a sudden I felt this, well, a kind of commitment to the bag and to tell you the truth, to Marge. After all, she'd gone to the trouble and, well you know.

In my tiniest, most immature voice, I whined, "How much is it?"

Now you need to understand, that I figured that this was not just a "designer" bag, but *couture.* I had just recently learned that word in my homework magazine assignments for my daughter. I was expecting that it was going to be so much money that no-way-in-hell would I be able to justify buying it. It would not matter how hard my new best friend Marge worked to search for it.

Clever Marge gaily answered, "M," I made note that I was no longer a "Honey" or a "Sweetie." We were now on first-name basis here, "I can't believe it, but it is just $785.00!"

I swear, she really said, "just" as if SEVEN HUNDRED AND EIGHTY-FIVE DOLLARS, was no biggie. Of course, since I fantasized that it would be up in the $3000+ range, suddenly, $785 sounds, well, *reasonable.*

Marge, extreme saleswoman, sensed my hesitancy and went in for the kill. Reassuringly, she purred, "Ya' know Honey; you can have the bag on *consignment.*"

I went dead on the phone. *Consignment? What does she mean?*

"So, ya' know, if ya' don't like it, just send it back." She could mine-read as well.

"Oh," I perked up, "that's. . . nice." I could get the bag. I could drape it on my slouchy shoulder, prance in front of a mirror, then come to my senses and chicken out, and send it back. No harm, no foul.

Marge paused on the line and added, "Of course, you'll have to pay the shipping, and Honey, I at this moment, I'm not really sure how much that would be."

By that time, I was on a consumer roll. Drunkenly, I thought, *shipping, no big deal. The Bag is Mine. Shipping, who cares?*

Within minutes, she had my credit card number.

Exactly twenty-four hours later, Fed Ex delivered a box that is the size of an end table. As I signed for it, I gasped; $85.00 in charges just to ship the damn thing. I started to think that I was headed into some deep cat poo here. But who cared when Jeremy and thousands of miles of Asian travel was involved? I tore open the box and I found the largest, roundest purse that I've ever seen in my life. Funny, it didn't look so, well. . . *round* in the magazine. Nor did it look so big. Of course, I forgot that models are nearly six feet tall, while I was barely over five feet, but still...

Don't get me wrong: it was spectacular: The leather was beyond luggage quality shaped into a flat semi-circle of architectural design perfection. The hardware was solid brass. This thing was first class all the way. Actually, it wouldn't get into first class. It was too damn heavy. It weighed in at seven and a half pounds, empty. That brass hardware, was all over that bag. It was like carrying around a baby on your shoulder. A *shiny heavy* baby.

Forget consignment. I was too committed to being fashionable and I admit it, too prideful to send it back to New York City where it really belonged. I took that bag to the big box store with me, not exotic locations. It went to the dry cleaners, and then back into its protective bag every night for fear of it getting scratched or wrinkled or angry. I draped it artfully on chair backs and watch in horror as its enormous weight pushed it to the dirty floor. It had to sit in the baby seat of the shopping carts because it was too heavy to hold and push a cart at the same time.

No matter, I still lugged the thing around, in a pathetic attempt to lope the way the models do, but my right side of my body kept listing down, down, down. I was at last, really slouching. Ultimately, I developed neck, shoulder, and hip pain. I went to my doctor. Clearly, I was in denial, refusing to even entertain the idea that The Bag could be causing my pains. My doctor who was only thirty-three greeted me on the examining table and scanned the room. Her eyes fell on my purse.

"Fabulous bag."

She walked over and ran a latex hand around the circular contours.

"May I?" As she lifted it to her shoulder, she asked, "Where did you get it?"

But before I could answer proudly or maybe shamefacedly, she barked, "Holy shit! This thing's a monster! Bet that's what's killing you." She dropped the bag like it contained radioactive material. "You've got Chronic Big Bag Spasm Syndrome."

"Is this a joke?" I growled. She hadn't even read my pre-appointment comments. *She was clearly jealous of my bag.*

"No," she sauntered over to me, pushed my head this way and that, and shook her hers as I winced. "I'm five six and weigh in at one-hundred-thirty and *I* wouldn't risk it.

"It's pretty common with your LV, Hermes, any of the Big Heavy Beautiful bags. I'm afraid this is going to have to go into the closet shelf for a while." When my face scrunched up in horror, she assured me, "at least until you get into a weight training program."

Needless to say, I didn't join the gym so that I'd be strong enough to schlep my couture bag around. Nor did Jeremy Irons come up behind me in the *grocery store*, which was a good thing, because I was usually very wrinkled and sweaty from carrying my Gigantic Bag everywhere.

After two more weeks of excruciating pain, and glimpses of myself in store windows, *The Short Woman with the Round Suitcase attached to her body*, I stopped carrying it.

At the nearly two-year anniversary of my buying the most expensive purse I ever owned, I gave it to the consignment store. Yeah, there's a whole other aspect to the word "consignment."

Six months later, I got a tax-donation check for *seventy-five dollars*, and a lovely note reminding me to think of them the next time I buy another over-priced beautiful bag. So much for self-love.

CHAPTER SIX

I'm A Former College Teacher, Damn It!
or
Great Job for Retired Persons or
Bored Housewives

MY HUSBAND DECIDED TO RETIRE EARLY. THAT IS TO SAY, earlier than *I* would have wanted him to. In the first two months of his withdrawal from the rat race, I really enjoyed having him home with me. It was fantastic to take early morning walks together, stop, and have coffee, talk about our past, and plan future excursions. We developed a cute little domestic routine: coffee, feed the dogs, breakfast on the patio, walk the dogs, coffee, and then we would both retire to our offices to write–and of course, continually pee due to all the coffee we drank.

Sometimes, like true retired folks, we took naps—in separate rooms. Well, that was part of the problem. At first, I'd lie down next to him, but I want to *read* at naptime, he wants to… well, *you know*. I mean, sex is great, but a nap is *so* nice. I'd hide out in the TV room. Then I'd feel guilty when I heard him inquiring, "Honey, are you ready for me?"

After a while, I was starting to feel that a spouse being home could really cramp one's style. The fact was the man was getting on my nerves. I really noticed it when *he* started to get restless and bored: he began to "fix things." Now my husband was very good at writing checks, not handiwork. We still have an upside-down screen door in the back of the house. My hose turner turns counter intuitively, there's a light switch that has to be hit several times to be "coaxed" into performing, and the sprinklers that he self-installed either leak weakly or explode periodically like Old Faithful.

I did what I could to *positively discourage* him without destroying his endearing creativity, but it was hard, ladies, really, really hard. I ended up spending hundreds of dollars, stealthily hiring repairmen at the rare intervals when my spouse would go out to yet another hardware store, to undo the massive damage to our home.

When he suddenly ceased to do any home-improvement projects, new problems arose. As I was leaving to meet a gal-pal for lunch and he'd comment:

"Wow, do you lunch *every* day?"

I could hear the silent accusation that I was abandoning him and going off to frolic while leaving him to nosh on last night's leftovers.

I glared back, defensively responding, "I meet the girls *once a week*, not *every* day."

"Seems like every day to me. You go out of the house almost *every* day." He shrugged and looked at his chest, making me feel horribly guilty over what, I don't know.

"I go to the grocery store, or the pharmacy, or the doctor, or the gym."

"Well, regardless, I'm here—*alone*."

So, I attempted to assuage my guilt by making him an entire lunch every time before I'd escape. After a while, he announced that he was really lonely eating his turkey-on-rye-with-cranber-ry-sauce-sandwich alone, could I join him before I departed to said nail, hair, shopping excursion?

At last, I found myself doing the unthinkable: inviting him along. Pretty soon, I was back into the carpool business: schlep-ping a family member around– my husband. He was joining me for lady's luncheons, baby and wedding showers. He stated proudly that he was now "one of the girls." And this was sup-posed to make me happy. It did not make me happy; but it did make me *crazy*.

Hubby was completely at ease with the ladies. At the luncheon, he didn't hesitate a second to jump right into the conversation, which proved to be a bit strenuous on my friends.

A girlfriend lamented that her sex-drive is-as-dead-as-a-rab-bit-ran-over-by-a-station-wagon-full-of-kids-jamming-down-the-highway, and my husband helpfully advises, "Buy a *really* big vibrator. I read in a magazine that at your age, a woman needs a bigger jolt." He gestures towards me, "M *loves* hers!"

"Uh oh, too much information Honey." I smiled until all the Botox in my nasal folds has been pushed out. I really tried to sound calm, but I was secretly planning how I could stuff a dinner roll down his throat to shut him up, but to no avail, five minutes later he was sharing info regarding my favorite soft porn ,which by the way is "Red Shoe Diaries" and of course *Fifty Shades of Grey*, one, two and three.

When he wasn't helping my friends with their sex lives, he was offering up counseling on child-rearing.

"I just always found it useful to ignore the negative behavior. That *always* works." And he should know, since *my* job was always the role of mean parent.

Regarding my lady friend's sudden, pre-menopausal weight gain, he brilliantly admonished, "Yeah, I'll say, you've really packed it on since that wine-lunch we had last week. Say, have you ever thought of joining our health club? It's great, you can go in the morning before you start any chores and–"

I interrupted him with a sharp thump on the shoulder, and hissed, "Husband, no! Sit! Stay! Quiet!" However, he was not quite done. He jammed in, quietly under his breath, but loud enough for the table to hate him, "or just don't eat anything."

"Uh, yeah Honey, that's real helpful. . ." I mouthed "I'm so sorry," across the assortment of glassware and sweets to my now-flushing, flashing, fat ex-friend.

Husband also accompanied us to chick-flicks, crying profusely while we looked around sheepishly embarrassed. That
is except for when we went to Fifty Shades of Gray, when he
spent the whole time snickering and whispering, "Yeah, like
you wish…" He joined me for my nail appointment, got himself
a pedicure and announced that, "This is really neat. Think I'll
do this every week. Do *you* go every week?"

I glared back at him and hissed, "No, I go every *three weeks.*"

"Why?"

"Because I have a low allowance."

I turned around and I saw that he was handing the manicurist a ten-dollar tip and she was salivating over his feet while
massaging them. I really did not like that adoring look she was
giving him.

I got especially prickly when I looked over and heard
her croon, "You wanna I give you extra-*long* massage?" And
Husband-who's–was going-to-be–tasered-when-we-got-back-
into-the-car, replied, "Oh…yeah…wow, *yes!*"

I changed salons after that day. Went to Alma the Hun. Six
feet four, grey dreds, no foot massages for men. She hates men.
I think she might actually *be* a man.

The following week, my spouse tried to follow me out the
door as I was leaving. I whipped around and nose-to-nosed
him. "What. Do. You. Want?"

He dropped his very nice looking eyelashes and implored, "I
thought I'd go with you."

I was strong. I was nasty. "Not today."

"Why?"

I hated lying to my husband, but I was trying to save our marriage and his life. "Because," I looked him right in the eye, "I'm going to the gynecologist."

Victory at last. Nothing freaks a man out more than the female-doctor scare or an assignment of purchasing sanitary pads. At last, I was able to go out alone–to the hairdresser.

The "closeness" thing was killing me. One day after eating together, drinking coffee together, walking together, going to the dry cleaners together, the market together, the hardware store together, the bank together and the dentist–together, I had enough.

I trounced into the kitchen and announced, "One of us is getting a job or someone is going to be killed."

Husband looked up at me and gave me what can only be described as a shit-eating grin and exhaled, "Well, go right ahead, I'm perfectly happy staying at home, in fact, I love it. I think I'm going to take a cooking course."

He kept his word and learned how to cook. I'm a fool; all those years, he should have been cooking. He was great.

I decided to look for work. Unfortunately, the "Other Lie", I had once believed, was that "with a college education and a major in English, you can always teach" (my mother, circa 1965), was proving unreliable. No teaching jobs were available and definitely none for mommies who had slid off the fast track in a careening mini-van for twenty years and now had perpetually grey roots that reappeared every five weeks.

I scoured the newspapers, e-lists, and followed up on every rumor I heard while standing in line at Starbucks. I was beginning to imagine that I might have to fire my Brazilian cleaning boy, Jack and take over his practice–after all, he made eighteen dollars an hour plus tip. I wasn't above cleaning houses; I'd done it all the way through college. I still knew how to weld a Lysol bottle and mop, but why would I do that? After all, I had that masters, degree, and those credentials. I wanted out of the house, and of course, some money for my trouble.

Then I saw an ad for retail sales in a very fancy shoe store. I had absolutely no retail experience but I figured that teaching is kind of like selling, you have to convince the customer (student) that this intangible thing (education) is worth "buying", so I thought I'd give it a shot. Besides, *I* wore shoes, which ought to be worth something as far as my credibility. Although I'd never owned a pair of *really* expensive shoes, I wished I did…

At any rate, with the help of one of my working-already-girlfriends, I tweaked my resume and sent it out. I really didn't have much hope. So, I was quite shocked when I was called in for an interview. I immediately faced some practical problems. I'd been living in my well-worn, comfortable jeans, tennis shoes and/or flip-flops for over a decade. When I tried on my old "business suits" (from my days as a principal) they were too tight and too long, which ominously suggested that I might be morphing into literally round ball. In addition, the jackets had shoulder pads that now made me looked like I was trying out for the NFL. I quickly jogged down to a discount fashion store where I bought a generic black suit, a pair of high-heeled pumps (more about those puppies later) and panty hose.

It took me five minutes to get the panty hose on. Apparently, fabrication had changed quite a bit. There was a lot more compression than in the old days. I remembered when panty hose actually contained nylon. Now they were mostly tensile-strength Lycra. On the way to the interview, my vaginal area went completely numb. This was good, because I had been worrying about having to nervously pee.

The interview went surprisingly well. This was in spite of the fact that I had tingling zings of pins from having my innards stacked and squashed by control top panty hose. My feet also were throbbing, although I had only been in my mid-size heels from the car to the building. There were warnings right then had I paid attention to them. But frankly, I was just too thrilled to have won an interview after my lengthy hibernation.

I tried to sound calm and blithely sophisticated as the interviewer fired off questions. At last, the session concluded, and she graciously offered me her hand, stating that I was "delightful and charming," and that she was sincerely hoping that there'd be a place for me at The Fancy Shoe store. As I stood up, she leaned forward and placed a plain, no polish, white-cuffed hand on my arm. She stared at my slim-fitting baby pink camisole under my cute fitted hot pink jacket that was skimming my pencil skirt and shook her head.

Graciously, she warned, "Of course, you understand that if we hire you, which I think we just might," she raised her hand and gestured towards my skirt, "you need to know that here, at The Fancy Shoe store, we strive for a more *sedated* look, and... (pregnant pause here), looser-fitting garments."

I blushed (more about this later as well) and shrugged my shoulders with Gallic indifference.

I answered, "But of course."

I was confused; I was wearing a *suit*. Admittedly, it was a hot pink suit, but I had thought this was a high fashion shoe store—trendy, young, and *fun*. I contemplated, *too close-fitting* as well the color of my outfit. *Pink is my downfall.*

At that moment, I actually looked around at my surroundings. We were sitting right on the sales floor at a little desk. I glanced at my cute apparently-too-tight-too-pink sleeve and thought, *I need to wear dark navies, dark gray, black, dark, dark clothes. I thought it was a fun store.* I studied the salesforce on the floor. Except for a shock of crisp white shirts, everyone looked like they'd just come back from the same funeral.

I waited for my phone call, really doubting that I'd get hired. I was pretty shocked when the interviewer stated that she "absolutely adored" me. In celebration, I joyfully went out and purchased three interchangeable boring dark suits.

It was the shoes I did not understand. I figured, "Hey, I'm going to be working in a *shoe* store; I'll buy my shoes there." I obviously hadn't bothered to check the shoes price tags (which by the way, were transparent and subtly, nearly invisibly, inserted deep inside the inner toe of our shoes.) This is done so we could separate the wheat from the shaft: those folks who had to squint, and extend their necks, while gripping the heel of the shoe, twisting it around, looking for the price, cannot afford our shoes. That is why they were actually *looking* for the price tag and therefore, we rarely had to bother with them at all. As they say in Retail Land, *"if you have to ask, you can't afford it."*

It was my first day at work and within two hours I was limping around the store. I discovered that I couldn't wear high heels to work. In fact, I couldn't wear high heels from the closet to my bathroom. I couldn't wear low heels. Possibly I could wear slippers, but maybe not, as every toe on my feet had a blister. My spider veins were starting to bulge into suspiciously looking like my Grandma Dorothy's varicose veins. I looked around like a stranded sailor on a raft: I was surrounded by shoes, but not one pair could I wear, not to mention that even with the discount, I couldn't afford any shoe in this store.

By three o'clock, I was eyeballing shoppers who came in, checking to see if they had on tennis shoes. If they did, I watched them like a lion with zebras, just waiting for someone to falter, so I could rip those shoes off their plumb feet. I'd hover as they removed their comfortable shoes to pull on our over-priced, beautifully made Italian creations. I contemplated a strategy for stealing a customer's old comfy shoes. I'd encourage the victim to wear her newly-purchase tortures "out." Then I would simply "forget" to put her old ones in the shoebox. I never did it, but the fantasy sustained me through hellish hours of agony.

We actually sold some fabulous and comfortable shoes. They were of course, fabulously over-priced as well. Our "cheapest" shoes were four hundred dollars a pair. We even had swanky "athletic" shoes. Of course, none of our shoes were manufactured in China or Taiwan. Nope, first of all, our shoes were never "made;" they were "fashioned" in Italy, France, or

Germany. "And each and every one," we assured our customer, "was hand sewn and signed by the *artisan.*" *Artisan,* code word in upscale stores for a "laborer." *That* word brings up visions of little children hunched over machines in dark factories, so it's never used.

Of course, *we* were not allowed to wear anything that remotely looked athletic or casual or comfortable. Our feet had to be "professional looking" at all times. Mine looked like they wanted to report me for abuse. Colleagues urged me to take a break and go buy support hose. I did.

Now I really felt attractive: I had a smooth expanse of rubber sheen encasing my throbbing legs. I had also developed a strange gimpy walk, because my right big toe was killing me, and I'd thrown my left knee out to compensate when trying to walk/limp.

The next day, I come into the shop with a ten-pound tote bag jammed with every flat pair of shoes I own. Eventually I did break down and buy what can only be described as "grandma" shoes. They technically are not actually *shoes*, more like thick stretch socks, made from some kind of industrial strength spandex-like material, trimmed in *genuine leather*, with a very unattractive low chunky heel and finished with a square box toe. They looked very comfortable and I looked thoroughly dumpy. The residual pain from torturing my feet lasted about a week, and then suddenly, my ugly shoes became my darling best friends. At last, I was able to smile.

Now that the feet were conquered, I faced the new challenges; *The Palace Intrigue of Retail*. There are secret clubs, rules, sub-culture and expected behavior that was implicit. It was pretty much like being a character in *Game of Thrones*. The Rules go something like this:

#1: It is important to find out, Who Is Important.

This is so you can take an important lunch with that important person. I assumed that "important people" would be our swanky customers. Nope. They were actually the people who have major influential power in your job. These shakers and movers were not necessarily management level. Some people who deemed themselves important, might not actually carry any weight as a genuinely important person. It got pretty damn confusing. For example, Marcos, was one of two people deemed capable of wrapping purchases. You see, our shoes didn't just come in a funky old shoe box. They come individually ensconced in a flannel bag, then lovingly laid down in a bed of wool, encased in a coffin of card board with bamboo trim, with our name emblazoned on the outside in bright plum with a Flemish gold font. Marcos could fuck-you up pretty fast if he slid into slow gear while one of your customers was anxiously awaiting their over-priced purchase; no doubt because they had a lunch date at an over-priced restaurant.

So, once I figured *that* out, I immediately made him some of Great Grammy's Oatmeal-Chocolate Chip cookies. I arrived early with my best china platter loaded with the cookies. Marcos took one look, shook his head and announced crisply, "I do not like cookies."

Crushed, I tentatively inquired, "Should I make something different?"

"Sí, bring Scotch."

"*Scotch*? Scotch cookies?"

He shot me a baleful look. "No, Scotch. Booze."

"Oh…"

As I turned to leave, he clarified, "Make it Macallan, single malt."

I was kind of taken back by that. "Err… is that expensive?"

"Sure, but you in sales, right?"

I had squinted down at him, "How much is it, Marcos?"

He shrugged his shoulders, took a sip of his coffee and grinned, "I think it's in the hundreds."

"Marcos, I can't do that," but I was thinking that maybe an expensive bottle of booze is a very good investment when you're waiting for Mrs. Fancy Pants shoes to get boxed. Thank goodness, he took pity on me.

"Okay, so get me *Glenfiddich*."

"Sounds pricey to me…"

"It's twenty-nine, ninety-nine at Price Wars, can you handle that? Jeez, you white ladies are so fucking cheap!"

He shamed me, so I opted for *Glenlivet 15* at fifty-three dollars and ninety-five cents. Once I delivered the "goods," Marcos and I were, well, best friends…kind of.

#2 The Operations people are in their own world and we are not supposed to enter it. EVER.

No sales consultant was supposed to go into the "other building." I think the operations folks liked their exclusivity and felt rather empowered by living in their secure island. They literally lived their lives covertly, working in an underground basement in a building actually adjacent to the store–with its own separate entrance, that was literally a half story below ground level. This added to the mystique of the wrappers who could wrap a pair of shoes in under five minutes and get them delivered to the sales consultant's trembling hands two minutes later.

To visit the area, as a salesperson, you had to have *good reason* and a clearance by a security guard. Hence, I had to make *two* plates of cookies if I wanted to see Marcos. These folks rarely got to see daylight. It took about ten minutes to walk to the elevator, wait for it, go in, and go up three floors, then walk across the showroom towards daylight. By that time, you've used up fifteen minutes of your hour lunch.

So, it made more sense just to travel the two floors and eat in their own lunchroom, which was in "basement #1" level. They work like blind hamsters, sorting, stacking, stocking, wrapping and hurriedly piling things onto our fancy delivery cart that one of them escorted up the elevator and personally presented to the customer.

One of our special presenters, Elsa, although working underground, was *way up* there in Important Land. She was a sixty-eight-year-old "retiree" who claimed, "They call me before holidays and they tell me come back, so okay, I'm back, but just three days a week, that's it!"

I think that she just couldn't keep away from shoes, or she too, had a crazy retired husband at home, I don't know. At any rate, three times a week she dawned a plum button up over-sized shirt, with her name embroider in our copy-write gold and she'd roll her cart out of the elevator to personally hand over our plum/gold bag, bursting with an explosion of plum tissue, to the anxious salesperson who would then, with great flourish, turned and handed it to the customer. Sometimes Elsa would by-pass the waiting salesperson and hand the package to the customer herself.

When this occurred, it was accompanied by her waving her left hand magically over the bag and with her right hand, shaking a finger with a gentle maternal warning, "Now don't forget to put these shoes back in their special bags at night! No shoetrees for our Fancy Shoe Store shoes. And keep the bamboo string, because it's good for presents later!"

Customers loved her numerous ideas for recycling our wrappings and boxes. It became quite a status symbol to have one's shoes personally delivered by Elsa, Herself. Some customers would actually wait an extra thirty minutes for Elsa to finish her lunch, so they could have her special presentation experience. Often, they'd ask if she was working that day, if not, you could lose a sale, as they'd assure you, "I'll come back later."

Clearly, our customers knew that Elsa was one of the "Really Important People."

I nurtured my relationship with the operations folks. And although my motives were not purely altruistic, as I quickly found out that the one person you didn't want to piss off was the person whose job was to retrieve a size 11 pair of shoes, buried deep in the bowels of the ten-foot-high stacks of boxes.

I really liked them. They were straight shooters. I'd come in early before opening, with a tray of sweetened coffee and dough-nuts, invite them to join me in the "upstairs" lunch room, a place not forbidden to them, but clearly not so desirable either. Sipping coffee with them was a calm and humorously succinct experience. Unlike the sales personnel who all had oral diarrhea, spending nearly all their chewing time, gnawing on their recent conquests or failures, the non-salespeople seemed to be folks of a few words.

"So, Doris, how's things in shipping?"

"Things good," munch, munch, "yep, it's OK."

"You have a family, Doris?"

"Sure, I gotta kids! I have three, all done with college and five grandbabies."

"Wow, that's great."

"Ya, it's good." She stood up, dumped her paper plate and announced, "Gotta go, to Operations now. You have a good day, M. okay? An' thanks for the sweets."

End of conversation.

I spent nearly all of my lunch breaks in the lunchroom, trying to tune out the complaining, the jealous speculations, the laments for better pay, bigger commissions, followed by mumbled threats to quit. As it turns out, salespeople are never very happy. It's the nature of the beast. It is what drives them to work harder, a kind of sick motivator for success. I would have loved to go out for lunch occasionally, but I figured out that with a twelve dollar a day parking fee, dry cleaning cost for the *ugly dark suits*, and the credit card bill for my comfy-clunky shoes, that I couldn't afford to eat out anyway.

#3: There is a bizarre, covert protocol of who is allowed to sell to whom and under which mitigating circumstances.

Try to imagine the salesperson as a kind of well-dressed hyena who stalks the customer as he/she enters the hunting territory. As soon as the sales person greets the customer with either a nod or an actual vocalization, the hyena symbolically pees on the unaware customer. This *marking* occurs without the customer ever being aware of it, save for the magic, cloying request that might sound like this,

"Hi, my name is Suzie-Got to-Pay-My-Saks-Bill; ask for *me* if you have any questions." Translate to: "You're *mine.*"

This is followed by a stalking motion that might look like a stroll to the casual observer, but is in fact done so closely that it's nearly up the customer's behind. Then the magic question is fired out, "What is *your* name?" This inquiry is not for politeness, it is to ID the victim for any outsider's attempt to mark the customer. Now Suzie can claim to "know" Mrs. Evans, to insist that she is in fact, "very good friends" or even better, Mrs. Evan's *sales-consultant-of-choice.*

As the customer perambulated around the room, and foolishly paused in front of *any* pair of shoes, the hyena would take a big inhale, and purr, "even if I am not here, *ASK* for me." Occasionally, one could catch the "old timers" actually chanting a subliminal mantra into a hapless customer's ear: "Ask for Suzie, ask for Suzie. Ask. For. Suzie." Often a small diminutive smile was added for effect and a self-effacing, "I'd really appreciate it."

#4: Once the customer had effectively been "tagged," all other sales consultants are to keep away from the marked customer.

We now knew that Mrs. Evans belonged to Suzie. The Suzie stink was on to stay; there was no rubbing it off. Even if the customer came in and mistakenly forgot to Ask-for-Suzie, it is practice to ring up that sale for Suzie anyway. The customer is no longer Mrs. Evans; she is *"belongs to Suzie."* It was a kind of sad watching the innocent customer absently nod and meander around, not noticing the wet spot on her skirt.

#5: When you "ring-up" a marked customer, you must give the entire sale to their owner, even if you spent an hour with her–and you better do it with a big old shit-eating grin on your face, as well.

If you failed to make good on this issue, chances are the offended salesperson will hunt you down, and gobble you up like an alligator grabbing a gazelle. No joke. If you unwittingly, ("really, I didn't know Mrs. Stuck-up was your customer. She *didn't ask for you*, she just wanted bedroom slippers.") ring-up a sale, you damn well better be prepared to "reverse it."

"Reversing" a sale involved, crawling to the Sales Manager and confessing that you knowingly or unknowingly "stole" Suzie's sale, that you were really, *really*, sorry and that you gladly give "back" your entire measly 5% commission to Mrs. Stuck-up's rightful owner, *Suzie.*

Yes, it was indeed painful to have worked over an hour with some old biddy, stroking her knobby, gnarly feet and ring up the commission for someone else. It just takes doing a good deed to the extreme. One only prayed that the recipient will remember your sacrifice and pay back in kind, that was mostly wishful thinking. Because the pay was mostly commission-based, it fostered a kind of Survivor Island mentality. And like the show, *you're not there to make friends.*

#6: Face up to it: everyone is out for a sale and unfortunately, there just aren't that many customers around, so it's going to be roller-derby time and someone is going to get a bump on the head. This translated to six or seven people swooping down on any poor soul who unwittingly entered our store to "just look." In our mode, there were no "just lookers," except for those who unwittingly looked inside the shoe for the price. And even those had *potential*, as we'd say. We would cajole, bully and hypnotized anyone foolish enough to cross our threshold.

I often chuckled to myself that the really good salespeople could "glamour" a customer–just like a vampire would prey, guiding the poor soul to give up her American Express card clutched in her trembling hands to the waiting talons of the sales associate. And then, like the victim whose neck was pierced, she'd look up, bleary-eyed, yet eager, as Elsa shoved a plum-wrapped confection of over-priced shoes into her limp arms.

Now don't get me wrong, I actually enjoyed my co-workers. Some of them were adorable in their own demented kind of way. Sometimes the whole thing reminded me of sixth grade, but other times the internal struggles were as epic as any soap opera or a play set in an archetypal castle.

The "palace" was full of complex characters, with layers of emotions and intentions. There was the single mom trying to supplement her ex-husband's sporadic alimony and child support checks. She hardly sold anything. She spent most of her time on the phone putting out crises at home, or at one of the kiddies' schools. She lucked out and met a divorced man with no kids who rescued her out of retail land. Everyone surmised that she'd be back in to shop, but wisely, she never did. I hope she's enjoying a life of carpooling, golf and wearing tennis shoes.

Then there was the aging bitter divorcee who got nothing except the ten-year-old cat, and the fifteen-year-old car. At first, I felt so badly for her, I practically handed over sales to her. Eventually, I realized that she'd mow anyone down without her old car, if you got in the way of a potential sale.

There were two widows who felt cheated by the shockingly low insurance payoffs and were forced to work so they could get a decent discount, and the ambitious clotheshorse whose commission checks merely chase her credit card payment every month.

One of the classic personas was *Anna Belle-the-Southern-Belle*. Anna Belle was fabulous looking. She was nearly six feet tall, slender and possessed what I thought was the best head of hair I'd ever seen and nearly flawless skin. No one has ever determined just how old Anna Belle really was. For all we know she may have had four face lifts and at least some of the time, that great hair, was actually one of several great wigs, sometimes supplemented by some spectacular hair pieces and extensions. She's been married four times, divorced four. The one constant in her life was her shoes and maybe her closet. She showed up before the security guard and left right behind him. She had to, because she would buy a new pair of shoes nearly every day and he had to check her bag, verify the purchase and often escort her to her 1998 Cadillac Coupe.

I had the misfortune of coming in too early one morning and caught Anna Belle fastening on her disguise. She actually arrived to work in a coat that could double as a possible zip-up bathrobe, a Hermés scarf wrapped around her head, *and* high-heeled boots. It crossed my mind that maybe Anna Belle had a "second" job in the evenings. Anyway, there she was in *disha-bille*, carrying a gigantic round case with her hair on a form. She had a head form that is an exact replication of not just her head, but facial features as well. She brought her own vanity chair and it resided in the ladies' room as an enduring fixture and homage.

She'd take a about a half hour to layer her make-up, while her curling iron heated up, then another twenty or so minutes securing her hair style of the day. By the time she was done, and she exited, carrying a hand-carved wooden head of herself, that creepily had eyes, nose, and blood-red lips. It was hard to determine who the mannequin was. The only give away is that the real Anna Belle was attached to a body.

Anna Belle was impeccable in her manners, but I was on to her. She would glide about the shop, greeting her co-workers who were always in awe of her, drawl in her deep Tennessee purr, "Well hel-lo darling. How are yu'all this morni'n'?" If you mistakenly replied that you were fine. Anna Belle would lean forward like a giraffe about to munch some grass and glare at you, then sneer, "Well, that's just *great*! What did you do, make a damn sale or something?"

I never quite understood what was bad about making a sale, but I guess if it wasn't *her* sale it was a "fuck you" to all others. Anna Belle was a true diva who worked only enough hours to earn a discount and absolutely refused to do anything unpleasant such as a nasty old return.

Many a day, one could hear her trill, "Now sugar, you can't *really* expect to return this, can you?"

She'd lean down and still tower over most customers, with all that hair looming over the pitiful customer and hiss, "Come on Sugar, you say you just *tried* these on?"

Guffaw, guffaw, huff, huff, "Hell, I dun' wanna make a *lair* out of ya'll, but I *know* you wore them out at least once, 'cause I saw you at the Gala last night and you had those," her long red finger nail pointed accusingly, "Christian Louboutin's right on those pink toes of yours!"

The fraud perpetrator would then skulk out of the shop in shame.

Anna Belle was at least a lady. She was the direct opposite of Sara-Screw-You-For-A-Sale-Or-Just-Screw-You-For-Fun. Sara was a blonde bombshell named Sara "Without-the-H," who wielded her cleavage the way a knight might swing a sword. We all basically just gave up ever trying to wait on any male customer unless he was gay. Gay men were terrified by Sara's large aggressive breasts and one inch false lashes. I think that straight men were scared as well, but too embarrassed to show it. That probably was why they'd purchase anything to get out of the store before their wives found out.

In the Male Competition, Danny-the-Shover, a talented fellow who could literally push you away from a customer at the counter by a subversive hip action. He could knock you to the ground quicker than a hand hitting you upside the head. Apparently, he also felt that he was obligated to monitor everyone's lunch hour, and so at any given moment he might burst out like a Turrets victim, 'Oh! Melissa is five minutes late from her lunch break!" or "I just noticed that Sara took an hour and a half morning break." He actually carried around a little black book where he recorded the following information:

His sales.

If he could find out, other people's sales.

Customers he had "marked."

Everyone's daily lunch schedule with a small hand-made spreadsheet of the *actual* break time vs. notated time gone.

A running tally of his favorite shoes of the day, week or month.

Sara didn't think much of him and was heard to say one morning, "That Danny is a horse's ass*hole*. And speaking of asses, he'd steal the crack right out from your butt if he could."

I don't know if she was correct, but it certainly was a profound word picture. I just mumbled under my breath something about "the pot calling the kettle black." I suppose that I was lucky that no one picked up on my witticism. I thought Danny was a really sharp dresser and even his Little Black Book was very chic—made out of crocodile and embossed with his initials in gold. *Swanky guy, that Danny. And he was witty too—regardless of his butt-crack thievery.*

We also had the store's own version of a *Menopausal Psycho Schizophrenic Scary Lady*. Her name was Hillary. One never knew what might happen with an innocent "good morning." It was mind boggling. She was a total charmer to customers, but was always glaring, snarling, or muttering to her work "colleagues." If there was a baby shower, wedding gift, or birthday bash, we'd draw straws to see which hapless person had to go solicit her for funds. Most of the time I steered clear of her potential wrath, but sometimes, feeling playful, I'd bait her by saying "Hi, top the morning to you Hillary." I'd wait until mid-day, after not one customer had drifted in and snidely confide, "I made *five* phone sales today." I was lying, but it was fun just to watch her turn red, make a fist and twirl her head in a spin ten times.

We had several young people who didn't have the slightest idea how they had arrived at this staid, sensible shoe store to work. One was a cute curvaceous blonde, not even twenty-one yet, who was continually being sexually harassed by old, and I mean, *old*, customers. One, known as the Crazy Slipper Man, had already purchased five pairs of slippers from her and hailed her by the salutation, "Blondie, how are you today?" The man would buy ten more as long as he could gaze into her limpid blue eyes or preferably drool profusely at her ass.

One afternoon, I heard him tell her as she was kneeling at his feet, that he got a pedicure every week just for *her*. She nodded her head in silence, but I know she was really swallowing a little bit of throw up just then. He brought her bagged lunches. Inside, were barely decipherable notes telling her that she was beautiful. He left her lamenting voice mails, assuring her that if she just said the word, he'd take her out of retail land. Since he was such a profuse purchaser, she figured that it was useless to complain to her manager, so she basically lived in terror, and checked the sales floor furtively for his entrance.

Finally, his unwanted intentions became so severe that *Blondie* was forced to buy a cheap imitation wedding and engagement ring set, fabricate an entire fiancée who was described as coming home soon, from his *special forces assignment as a trained assassin from Afghanistan, as soon as he finished is psychiatric rehab regarding his temper.* Slipper man was relentless. Blondie then invented a wedding and married life, just to keep Crazy Slipper Man at bay. After two months of him ceasing to show up twice a week, she was seen collapsed in the lunch room, twisting the rings her of left hand and exhaled, "Omigod, maybe I won't have to wear this *Creep-Away* ring anymore!"

Other youngins welcomed the flirting, no matter the marital status of the customer or age. Alex, just barely twenty-three, bragged that she'd been out with four out of every six customers she waited on. If they're were males, make that six out of six.

The management team was pretty good: energetic, healthy and why not, they had a wonderful attitude about life because *not* one of them was a day over forty. I always felt like my kids were telling me what to do, what to wear, or how to talk. My own kids didn't hesitate to tell me that they at last, felt vindicated, knowing that someone as young as them was bossing *me* around…

I really felt badly for our six managers. It seemed like a very overwhelming job to oversee this carnival of weirdo-sales folks. I did notice with few exceptions a striking resemblance amongst all of managers. In fact, eventually they all just morphed into the same prototype as if they too, had some guidelines, albeit, unspoken ones.

1. *Managers, both senior and junior have absolutely no social life. This is pretty obvious since most of them arrived before we did, at around 7:00 am and were still hunched over their very nice wood desks once we had departed at 9:30pm.*

2. *Female's bodies must be shaped like a fireplug. Every managerial woman had a kind of square-bodied, Sponge-Bob look to them. In other words, they were built like mini linebackers which was probably necessary in order to break through the retail glass ceiling.*

3. *Male managers need to be emaciated, metro-thin. This rule applies whether or one is gay or not. They wear very spiffy clothes and nice shiny shoes and always, pocket squares.*

4. *Both genders own at least three Brooks Brothers Suits in the exact same color. If it was a female, then the skirt falls unflatteringly into the middle of the leg, making the short legs look even squatter. Males were expected to have cuffed pants, thereby enhancing the chance that their shoes would show. Oh and of course, managers, like their surfs below them, could only wear The Fancy Shoe store' shoes,*

no Shoe Pavilion for them. In addition, it was expected that Mangers shy away from "sexy" style shoes, and show a more staid, practical, i.e., our uglier line, of shoes. I overheard a vice president admonishing a manager that "We are not selling sex here, we're selling shoes. Just shoes." When she argued that the store sold some very cute shoes that were feminine, he just shook his head and replied, "You and the others, are to wear the Other. Kind. Of. Shoes. Get it?"Most female managers seem to be cursed with "piano legs ", which actually go well with mid-leg hems and those grandma shoes anyway.

5. Managers never wear denim. They must all appear to be uncomfortable, stuffy, not real, even on off-site work "party" events–even the company picnic. It was sad to see people sweating in slacks at the boat pond, hiking at the beach picnic in their Dockers.

6. Apparently, if not an unspoken rule, there was a company discount at some chop shop beauty salon because most of the lady managers sported a Peggy Fleming Haircut circa 1980. I guess it was just something they were issued during the management-training program and they all just stuck with it. Males had Peggy Fleming hair too.

7. The majority of the management team female squad had a slash of a mouth, faintly framed by thin lips, very red lipstick and topped with an endearing well-established blonde mustache.

8. *All had short man-hands, except the males had soft girl-hands. Who needs hands in the shoe business anyways? Needless to say, no nail polish. Hands are not to be a distraction. Hands are not to be sexy, just tools for tying shoes laces.*

9. *Apparently, large square feet were a manager requirement— good for standing on as one marched around the sales floor managing things.*

10. *Managers need the ability to generate two publicly announced boring memos a day. Sometimes one actually read from his family Bible, one from Emily Post, or a "thought of the day."* I barely had any room in my head for my own thoughts, let alone someone else's; I personally would rather have had "Pat the Bunny" read out-loud once a week. I've found very deep meaning in that little story.

In spite of their stomping around the sales floor, squinting over spread sheets of sales vs sales goals, the management team had no clue what the sales folks were up to. Managers were always stressed, clutching those reports in their sweaty, square, trembling hands. Sales people got the message: *sell lots and lots of shoes*. And we did, to every walk of life imaginable. Now you'd think that a swanky-fancy shoe store filled with somber funeral-dressed employees would intimidate the hell out of some customers. Nope, it was just not so. Turns out that we were so warm, ingratiating and friendly that we were able to attract not just the hoity-toity who only wore very expensive handmade shoes, but also everybody from, excuse the pun, all *walks* of life.

Feet. Well, I will tell you that a smelly foot knows no economic or social boundaries. I found out that even nicely dressed people could have very stinky nasty feet. I spent a lot of time rubbing liquid antiseptic hand cleaner on my hands, and then covertly leaving them slightly damp in hopes of disinfecting the scary feet. I just ignored customers who'd jump out of their seat and gasp, "What in the hell is that? Why are your hands cold, damp and sticky?" I'd smile and shrug and sell them an extra pair of shoes just for fun.

Once there was a dapperly dressed man who kept motioning me with his fingers to come hither. He was using that infamous middle finger to do his gesture. It was our pre-holiday sale and we were swamped. The man continued to make his finger gesture, and now was literally making some weird hissing sounds as well. I looked up, acknowledged him, as I tilted my chin towards the pile of six shoeboxes strewn on the floor. I was assisting a demanding, but regular customer, so I wasn't about to just jump up and run over.

I assured him, "I'll be with you as soon as I am done, Sir."

Finally, I concluded my sale and rushed over to the hissing, finger-wiggling, and now, hand-waving man.

He leaned across the counter and said in a meticulous British accent, "Madame, I've been *fingering you for ten minutes now* and *you did not come!*"

Oh boy, let me tell you about biting one's tongue. Under my breath I murmured, "Well it takes more than *fingering* Sir."

Apparently, "fingering" is another word for hailing you for your attention. That line got my attention, that's for sure. I replayed that tidbit several times that day and nearly peed in my pants each time.

Our customers were mostly nice folks. These included some grandmas who were convinced that their feet could only feel comfortable in expensive shoes, lots of working girls like me who'd pay anything to make the throbbing pain stop and of course, the upscale, well-taken-care-of rich brats. This group came in all ages and sizes. Some were ancient divas who really enjoyed looking down (literally) at service people, showing simultaneously glee and distain that a "clerk" was touching their precious feet. Others were young women who'd never worked a day in their life and never would, thanks either to Daddy's money or Sugar Daddy's wealth.

We were supposed to write thank you notes to anyone who spent more than four hundred dollars and that covered just about every customer. Sometimes it just pained me to write those notes. Some people were just so damn rude, they didn't deserve a nice note of gratitude. What they *deserved* was something like this:

From Fancy-Shoes Incorporated

Dearest Ms. Peabody-Snotnose,
Thank you for giving me the honor of handling and smelling your gnarled gross feet. I especially enjoyed you referring to me in the third person while you chatted on your cell phone, and the way you signaled me to come over and "wait on you" immediately once you got off the phone. I hope you enjoy

your new shoes, you rude hideous old bitch. I sincerely pray
that they kill you with pain.
Please let me know if I can help you with any further useless
purchases.

Sincerely,
M, MA, ED BA
P.S. Yes, you hag, That's right! I'm twenty times more educated
than you are, even if I am stuck making $12.00 an hour and
touching your feet—all because my retired husband was driving
me crazy.

I refrained from actually mailing these but every now and
then I did have fun writing them out during my lunch break. I
had to make quickly for the shredder before anyone read them
over my shoulder.

I continued working at the shoe store until my husband
relented and got another job and the last daughter, Thing Two,
graduated from private college. I didn't mind working, after all,
it was for the Love—of my family, and I guess, shoes. Oh, I *did*
eventually did buy a couple of more pairs of those comfortable,
un-sexy shoes too.

CHAPTER SEVEN

Extreme Makeovers, Part A

I JUST WANT TO SAY THAT IN THIS CENTURY, I FEEL THAT there is absolutely no truth that one can grow old gracefully. Media and its celebrities won't let you. I say that because even the *older* stars, all look terrific due to plastic surgery, personal yoga instructors, and the wonders of photo-shop. In spite of the claims, I do not believe that a certain star's "pure water" has magical abilities. Either you fight back, or you cave in, and wind up shopping at a discount box store for muumuus, support panty hose and roomy pants. As a result, I spend every waking hour that I am not running errands, cooking, cleaning or working, on my poor beleaguered body that just wants to grow fat and get wrinkled. *But I will not allow it.* No way. Yes, I admit it. I suffer from FOGO, aka, Fear of Getting Old, and so what? They've extended our life expectancy, so who-in-the-hell wants to hang with well, hanging skin?

Let's start with what I will just call, The Very Popular Landfill Diet. Both my husband and I were, as they say gently, "putting a little poundage on." More like, we were busting out of our vintage jeans and careening dangerously towards the relax-fit status. I got *The Book.* This is how we referenced it in our house. It was in fact, the new family bible. It was an incredible diet. It really worked. There was only one problem. I haven't planned, let alone, actually *followed* a menu or recipe in nearly twenty years. Let's face it, after a while your family doesn't care what kind of slop you lay on the table as long as it has twenty-six grams of fat and tastes like French fries, even if it's roasted chicken.

So, I first spent days reading The Book. The Book was not just a cookbook—it was a philosophical guide, full of support, values and oh yes, *recipes.* It also had a mandatory two-week starter menu plan, followed by a *rest-of-your-fat-ass-life* menu guide. I studied it and didn't find donuts on it anywhere. I looked into the appendix for cupcakes. I found them, made with potato flour. I knew there was going to be trouble. After hours of studying, I felt like the fashion magazine study-guide all over again, I wrote down the forty-five new ingredients that I needed to own before preparing my chemically balanced nutritional meals. Foods only with low "glycemic indexes" – that basically don't have much sugar–or taste, are allowed. For example, fun cereals like rice bran, or gosh, that fun *all-bran*, are allowed. Or you can really go crazy and try to find at the local-communal-hippie-hemp-co-op-food store, some *pearled barley*. Hey, if you have to ask, you don't deserve to eat it. But here's a hint, you'll find it along with other tasty-sounding grains like "bulger." You can also just feast on the following:

Low fat, artificially sweetened yogurt—but not if the sweetener is saccharin, it has to be one of the new "extracts" of pineapples, or palm trees, I can't remember which plant

Boiled soybeans

Boiled red lentils (that's always been one of my favorites)

Artichokes until you choke

Arugula, a slightly bitter, but "lively" green

Kale, a *really* angry, jealous, vengeful green

Quinoa, high in protein, low in everything else, including taste. The price has been driven so high that the Bolivians who really depend on it, can't afford it. I'd like to give back to them immediately; "Here, take your tasteless grain back, please!"

Cabbage. This item is used several ways to fool one into thinking one is having some "fun" carbs.

Young summer squash. Apparently one must avoid the *Old Fall Squash*.

Nonfat whatever–does not include ice cream–don't even think of it. There is a "fake" ice cream that you create with ricotta cheese and vanilla flavoring that after a while, does taste good, because you've been so deprived.

After I had made my very expensive trip to the grocery store, (let's face it, good food cost money, tasteless food, even more), I then had to chop, slice, dice, smash and mix the biologically balanced ingredients. Not only did I have to *think* about what we were going to eat for breakfast, morning snack, lunch, afternoon snack, dinner and a so-called dessert, I had to *worry* about it. Besides the three strategic meals to plan, there are *three* Very Important Snacks, as well. If you were not going to be home, then you had to pack your snack and your lunch or strategize where you'd be eating out. I hadn't ever thought about packing snacks for me, or my hubby. Snacks were for kindergarten kids, right? However, I was committed to getting back into those maligned jeans of mine, so I soldiered on, in a low-carbohydrate way, of course.

The first two weeks of the menu and food prep was intense. The doctor who wrote the book repeatedly reminded us that this was a *chemically balanced* diet, and that if I didn't stay tried and true, I'd be responsible for my husband and me continuing to be fat-asses. Believe me, even guilt wasn't a good enough motivator for some aspects of this diet. One "no-no" was caffeinated coffee. Now decafe is great after a lovely late-evening dessert, preceded by three glasses of red wine. It just doesn't do the trick for five o'clock in the morning wakeup call. I spent the first three hours of every morning sleep walking, which was great, because that way I wasn't hungry.

There was also the snack issue. I was supposed to get excited over my two snacks for the day and feel *full*. It was a challenge. Could *you* get worked up over the anticipation of having one damn non-fat cheese stick at eleven-thirty in the morning? What exactly is a cheese stick without fat? Sometimes the wrappers tasted better than the contents. Afternoon snack was really a thrill consisting of more cheese, this time disguised in wedges, accompanied by a stalk of celery. One does learn to chew one's food slowly, when you are rationed down to a stalk of celery every afternoon. Sometimes things got really sexy and wild. *The Book* would step it up to cucumber rounds with salmon. Occasionally we were allowed to really veer off the road and have hummus accompanied by raw vegetables. Whew, ex-citing.

The cruelest prohibition was the bread no-no. I'm Jewish. Bread is part of all three of the basic food groups. I once made two loaves of bread with my bread maker and when my husband came home, his nose twitching at the fabulous aroma of bread-a-baking, I had to drop to my knees and confess that I had single-handedly consumed two loaves of piping hot bread. I had the burn marks on the roof of my mouth to prove it. Now I was supposed to not even look at bread, even *wheat* bread for two damn weeks. I'm sorry, but cabbage leaves are not an acceptable substitute for starchy French bread. And how come all the French women look slim and eat French bread? I tried to accept the fact that smashing up cooked cauliflower, surrounding it with *one-half* of a teaspoon of olive oil and calling it "tasty mash potatoes" was "just the same as mash potatoes," but it was not. It *was* funny, and weird.

Everything was served as if we were eating at a "tapas" restaurant–little pathetic plates of nothing everywhere. And during the preparation of the food, the only unit utilized was either a teaspoon or now and then, a tablespoon. Hence meals served looked more like what my daughter might have prepared for her Barbie dolls, not adult humans. Speaking of which, not once did my dog voluntarily step up to clean our plates with her tongue. She'd sit at my feet until serving time, then toddle over to the dinner table, wiggle her nose and walk away, head dejected in disgust. Sometimes, we'd walk away the same way. Of course, that was after *we* licked the plates, since the portions were so meager.

Dessert brought more feelings of dissatisfaction. The most popular concoction was the creation of a kind of frappe, fashioned out of ricotta cheese, four or five slivered almonds and are you ready? *Six* chocolate chips. I mean, it was actually fairly tasty, but come on, bring on the entire bag of chips and then maybe, just maybe, you'd have a *real* dessert. Ricotta cheese? Best as one of my three cheeses layered lasagna.

Perhaps the cruelest prohibition was the alcohol; which covered every kind of spirit including wine. Now this was really devastating. I craved my Cab, my Pinot, my Malbec. More importantly, I missed my moderate buzz that prevented child abuse and husband-killing. Instead, we were to drink water–lots and lots and lots of water. We were allowed home-carbonated water, sans sodium. Bubbly water became the go-to liquid treat of the day. I got so desperate I actually guzzled some red wine vinegar.

In spite of all my whining, my husband's pathetic whimpering, and the dog's refusal to lick our plates, we kept faithful to the program. I tried not to weigh myself every night–but I wanted to see some results for my suffering. Sometimes I'd wait until my husband was asleep and sneak over to our scale which cruelly was branded, "Thinner." It wasn't promising anything, it was just flat. Slowly, my husband and I began to lose weight. Our meals became relaxed and calm, that was due to the fact that Thing One had temporarily moved out. She did this as soon as she noticed that I wasn't having my "calm-me-down" glass of vino, to live at her best friend's house. Thing Two also refused to eat dinner at our house anymore, declaring that until our "mental illness" was over, she'd be eating every evening at Grandma's. I kept thinking of my children each night, while my husband and I sat alone in our dining room; wondering how tasty my mother-in-law's fried chicken-with-ham-hocks-flavored green beans might be?

I think we would have lost weight because we were urinating every two hours from the gallons of liquid we consumed. We ate small meals, frequently. Small breakfasts were easy, especially when one is looking down at a bowl of sugar-substitute oatmeal as one's morning treat. We became very fond of all kinds of almost-really-cheese: string cheese, low-cal cheese packs, cottage cheese and our dear friend, non-fat Ricotta. It was a happy cheesy time for everyone.

Within thirty days, we both had lost twenty pounds and we looked great. Well, my husband did. I had a bit of a problem. My loosing fat had left a sloppy skirt around my tummy and my thighs slapped together as I walked. I'm a woman of action, so I joined the gym. I lifted weights. My arms got big, but firmer. I started speed-walking, then running. I had to wear two bras to keep my poor saggy boobies from flying over my shoulders, but I gamely ran on. Problem was, that I ran in the early morning hours and my trip home ran me right by The Happy Donut Shop, renown for the best donuts in the city, and unfortunately, open twenty-four hours a day. It just didn't feel right running two miles, and then eating two donuts, so I stopped running. Of course, I never dreamed of changing my route, nor leaving the donuts. Besides, the donut aroma was accompanied by numerous other yummy temptations in the neighborhood including the bagel shop, two bakeries that made fantastic croissants and cupcakes, three restaurants that served sky-high-calorie-high pancakes from seven in the morning, not to mention, the latte shop with its *caffeinated,* whole milk beverages.

I decided to remove myself from temptation–I started using the stair-climber until my knees started popping. When they got to the crackling stage, on the advice of a friend, I took spin classes. My too-fit-too-cut-too-much-younger-than-I friend, Jeanette, could not praise the classes enough. "Oh, you're going to *love* the Spin class–it really kicks your ass! I get so much more in one hour than I *ever* did just running."

The "really kick your ass" part should have been the heads-up for me. Need I say more? Spin class, (pedaling faster than a hamster-on-methamphetamines-on-bike-that-goes-no-where,) is the ultimate in extreme exercise where you literally sweat out two gallons of water, hyperventilate and if you're really lucky, get to be humiliated by some twerp in biking shorts that shows his male organs barely encased in spandex and ass-crack every time he kneels down to adjust his IPod.

My guy, James, AKA, "Dr. Death" –I'm not kidding, that was his moniker. He was a former marine who took his job a little too seriously. For example, he would take his size twelve shoe, and jam it into my bike wheel, thereby slowing my pace to an unfathomable up-hill climb equal to sloughing up the Matterhorn. He'd do this and bark out in his gravelly voice, "Now peddle! Push hard!" He'd to this to the accompaniment of hard rock group Nine Inch Nails screaming, "I Want to Fuck You Like an Animal," while sneering, "Come on Bitch, do you want a fat saggy ass all your goddamn life?"

Once, in a small, teeny-tiny voice, I foolishly protested, "Please don't use that language and that music is really gross."

Big mistake. "*Gross?* You think the *music* is gross? How about those thighs slamming against the seat, isn't that *grosser?* Like, maybe even *über* grosser, eh?"

Great, now I was being insulted in *German.* I wasn't even sure if there was such a word as "grosser," but I decided to refrain from correcting his bad grammar. Good thing because he apparently wasn't even close to being done with me. He turned to the other savages on bikes and sneered, "What do you all think? What sound do ya'all want to hear, Nine Inch Nails or M's," he pauses and sneered at my legs, "flabby thighs?" The Skinny Asses chanted in unison, "Not M's thighs! Kill them before they multiply!" Suddenly, I was no longer in the gym. I was in *Lord of the Flies.*

Ugh, what a nightmare. What is absolutely amazing is that I *paid* to have this done to me. Not to mention, getting up at 5:00 am to phone the gym to get on the coveted "list" for Dr. Death's class. After a while, I just wasn't man enough. I dropped out. Actually, I *ducked* out because from that day forward, I had to hide from anyone who 'd been in his class because the guy had a cult following like Jim Jones.

I'd hurriedly scurry by the gym before one of his disciples could corner me and inquire with a serious concerned frown, "M, why haven 't you been to class?"

"It's not a *class*, it's a *session*, you don't actually learn anything, just how to sweat." I'd hiss back defensively.

"No need to get nasty. It's just that we all missed you, and Dr. Death was very concerned about you."

I bet. Concerned about who he planned to torture next. For a while, I had to avoid my own local market for fear of the Believers stalking me and grabbing my Sara Lee's out of my shopping cart, throwing a dirty gym towel over my head and kidnapping me back to the smelly gym for some re-programming. It wasn't that I was lazy, I was just, well, maybe a *little* lazy and kind of unfocused. I mean, even while I was in the spin sessions, when Dr. Death wasn't jamming his foot up my butt or into my bike wheel, I did have the tendency to drift off and well, plan my lunch menus, dream of sandwiches, or imagine my jogging over to the Happy Donut, that sort of thing. I guess my glazed, donut-infested eyes, were too easy to read. It was a shame, really, because I had designed some awesome sandwiches during those workouts.

After a week's hiatus, still determined to firm up, I enrolled in yoga classes. Yoga I thought would be relaxing. It is not. It is also a completive sport, where the youthful bend and twist themselves into exotic poses whilst the aged, over fifties, try to stay vertical with one foot ducted taped to a pleated thigh. I was getting discouraged. I could feel something happening under the fat. I was developing muscles, but still, that floppy skin thing was going on. When I walked, my inner thighs continued slapping each other ruthlessly. I could hear the followers in Dr. Death's class chanting in my head.

My tummy skirt still played peek-a-boo with my chunky-but-firmer-thighs. Now I noticed that I had some saggy jowls where my chubby cheeks (facial) use to be. The face thing started to frighten me. I mean I didn't think Dr. Death had a class for Face. I've didn't really strive for perfection, but I also didn't want to slip down the hill of imperfection. I wanted a balanced look, aging, but. . . err...ageless. It was expected that as my natural face started to naturally sag, that I'd take serious un-natural action.

Let me back up a bit–and watch out, because my butt has not had work done and it makes quite a dent in the backing-up department. I used to like myself–even my paunchy little tummy and my chunky thighs. The stomach was my badge-of-courage that I had survived the birth of two children and the thighs, well, it proved that I had survived countless interactions with Haagen-Dazs ice cream. It was just that weight loss thing that had triggered a shock effect. Oh, and along with a mistake I had made; I had purchased one of those 10x magnifying mirror because it was getting harder and harder to pluck my eyebrows. I now could see numerous stray hairs under my brows. I also discovered that they were gray, and that I had pores the size of Mt Vesuvius. My smile "lines" were not lines. They were crevasses. I was revolted. Where was my love? Why did I look so forsaken? Where was my love for *me*?

CHAPTER EIGHT

Part B: Expressing Myself through Botox and Restylene and Other Violent Methods

LIKE A STEALTH BOMBER, I STARTED SHOPPING AROUND for someone who could restore me into a semblance of the woman I once was. I'd stop strangers on the street, compliment their clothes, and then brazenly ask, "Say, you look terrific, have you had any work done? If so, by whom?" This had about a 10% success rate. Either they snarled at me to "bug off" or threatened to run me down with their shopping cart. I bought beauty magazines that highlighted Doctors of the Year. I decided to visit each one for a consult. Let me tell you that is no cheap ticket. Just to chat with these doctors cost the patient between seventy-five to hundred and fifty dollars a visit. Usually they generously offer to rebate the money if you signed on for the surgery. But at this point it was like applying for college entrances with all those application fees.

I was sitting in the slickest waiting room I'd ever seen. It could have been a set out of a TV show starring an upscale doctor who had movie star good looks and a reception area full of Barbie doll "gals." They could only be identified as "gals" as these persons were neither girls nor women–just, well, *gals*. Each was over five foot eight. All of them had long straight, shiny hair that was blonde, black or red. They all appeared to be a size two bodies with size ten breasts, and perfect little up-turned noses, all done by Dr. Feel Good himself. How did I know this? Because they each wore a button badge with their name and a slogan, "Like my nose? Ask Dr. Feel Good." Or, "Like my boobs, my eyes, my ears, my butt?" The receptionist breathlessly informed me that there would be a bit of a delay because Dr. Feel Good was actually a *patient* today and *his cosmetic surgeon was visiting him at his office for his post-op assessment.*

That's how I found, well, let me call her, Dr. Fix-it. Dr. Fix-it was allegedly over forty, but she didn't look a day over thirty. I watched her glide into Dr. Feel Good's office, dialogue with the "gals," and then sashay her way down the hall, tight buttocks beautifully displayed in her slim St. John pant suit. All of the gal-heads swiveled enviously towards, Dr. Fix-it's recently lifted derriere. It was war of the blondes at that moment. Dr. Fix-it looked like a classy version of a Play Boy Bunny.

In about ten minutes she glided out, followed by a cacophony of gal-giggles and whispers. A pert brunette with a sleek bob haircut and dangerously stained blood-red lips, summoned me.

"The Doctor will see you in his office."

"Oh, no exam?"

"Doctor likes to keep things comfortable. Less shocking."

Huh? Shocking?

She escorted me to a six-foot high redwood door. She knocked. Dr. Feel Good called me in. He was hot. Yes, even swollen from his "recent" surgery, he was gorgeous. In fact, he was *so* good looking that I decided to see *his* plastic surgeon. Without regret, I bagged my visit, left my hundred dollars behind and ran down the hall, hoping to catch my future savior. I got out of the elevator in time to see her take off in her Porsche, top down, but a jaunty baseball cap giving her adequate sun-protection. I was wasting no more time; quickly I snapped open my cell phone, connected to her somewhat snotty receptionist and gave her my credit card for a consult.

Upon my first official meeting with her, I knew she was crazy and my kind of woman. I opened the door to the examining room. The doctor was already there waiting for me. She didn't notice I was there because she was busy self-injecting her lips with Restylane. Her right hand was holding the syringe; her left was death-gripping the wall. She muffled-moaned, "Oh, hello Darlink. I didn't know… they were going to…" she paused, waiting while her eyes rolled back into focus, and then exhaled, "put you into this room." Any fantasies that I had about a relatively painless procedure such as filler injections were put to sleep when the doc cried out, "Oww! Oh-mi-god, that hurts!"

I just stood in the doorway. Now *I* was gripping the frame, in utter horror. Finished with the self-torture, Dr. Fix-it whirled around and gave me a brilliant, but teary-eyed smile. Her lips were already starting to morph into duck-lips. Beyond that I could see that she was absolutely darling. She lifted her heavy lashed eyes and stared at me with her bizarre piercing emerald green eyes. Her moonlight blonde hair, (definitely a recognizable color-job by a well-known colorist in our city) fell into fantastic soft waves around her perfect jaws. She had huge, perky breasts. I later discovered that the "perkys" were a pro-bono perk, as a curtsey from Dr. Feel Good. Her size-four or maybe even a two, sheath dress glided over her flat tummy and high-up-there ass without one line or pucker anywhere. Her neck and face were perfect. I hated her. I wanted to *be* her.

Her biography, detailed in a complex website, stated that she had graduated from Harvard medical school. She did her residency in cosmetic surgery, then she went to Stanford for more medical degrees. She was twice married and twice divorced. I figured that anyone as busy as she was making and spending money and looking so gorgeous had no business trying to be somebody's wife. I knew she had birthed three children and was at least forty-six years old and I envied her because she had birthed three children and was at least forty-six years old.

She handed me a mauve examination gown that was better looking than any lingerie that I owned, while explaining, "I just had to get this done today. I'm leaving for the Caribbean on Thursday and I absolutely don't trust anyone with my face but me."

She chuckled, "Well, sometimes, Dr. Feel-good, but he's so busy right now. It's breast implant season."

She absently dabbed a gauze pad at her upper lip that was oozing blood. She laughed and added, "He did my face lift, but only because I couldn't do it myself."

She looked genuinely frustrated that she hadn't been able to knock herself out and crank-up her own skin. I joined her with self-conscious laughter, nodding my stupid head stupidly.

Abruptly, Dr. Fix-it stopped laughing and became all business. She leaned against the soft-calming mauve laminate counter and pointed, "You need to strip. Now, *darlink*, now."

I blushed and unbuttoned my jeans in slow motion. She had this weird kind-of Hungarian accent, or perhaps it was that she was trying to speak through her duck lips?

I had frozen, clutching my wadded-up jeans and panties and mumbled, "I, err, the nurse just told me to go in here and wait for a *consultation* and–"

Dr. Fix-it, also known as Marianne, waved her perfect unwrinkled, no sun-damaged hand and gaily interjected, "Oh, vell now, no worries. Don't be shy, darklink. I can't consult without you bare, yes?"

She paused staring at my now half naked body, the gown and crumpled barrier between my saggy belly and her piercing green eyes. "So now, you need to take *all* the clothes off and put that on, and hop up here." She patted the examination chair that looked like it was covered in skin as nice as hers.

She focused on my floppy thighs and added, "If you cannot *hop*, then you use the step stool right there." She nodded to the elegant step stool and shook her head, then turned away from me.

I watched her as she walked over to the mirror on the wall and started pinching her duck lips into a more elongated version of well, goose-lips. I dropped my jeans, scooped them up and quickly folded them. Then I did something so ridiculous. I actually turned away from her and removed the rest of my clothing while awkwardly trying to unfurl the one hundred percent Egyptian imported cotton gown.

I barely got the thing over my head when she purred, "So, vhat brings you here?" She was now facing me. She frowned as I struggled to "hop on" the chaise lounge sans the cute lavender step stool that was near the table. Shaking her head, she gently pedaled the table down until it was six inches off the floor. I noticed that she had on pointy beige Jimmy Choos. No doubt, I'd be paying top dollar to add to her shoe collection.

Dr. Fix-it, sighed and gazed at what looked like a mini-computer in her hand and a camera in the other. I mumbled something about my body and she glided over. A French-manicured fingered gently prodded between the elegant frog-closures of my meager covering. She kept tilting her head sideways, poking at my rolls of fat. She looked like she was about to frown—well, at best, tried to frown with twenty liters of Botox in her forehead.

I felt like I should say something, so I ventured, "I think I need liposuction or a tummy tuck?"

"Or a face lift," she added, gently grabbing my jaw. Tugging painfully on one of my chins, she looked deeply into the souls of my brown eyes and shook her head. Barely whispering, she inquired, "You think you need to do something about your body?"

"Well…yes…I mean, ah, actually, I have been exercising for three months now and I lost twenty-five pounds and–" I was starting to tense up, feel inadequate, as if I should be searching for the right answer to an unknown question. I looked down at my belly, but she kept a firm hand on my jaw.

"M, is it? Uh huh, well my precious,"

My precious? What was up with that? Wasn't that a line out of Lord of the Rings? *What was up with the Gollum questions and the perverted duck-lipped Hungarian accent?* I didn't remember Hungry as a country of origin on Dr. Fix-it's bio, but maybe you could have an accent *implanted* as well.

Marianne released my face and stood back staring at me like a blank canvass–well a bumpy one maybe. She bit what would have been her bottom lip and exhaled, "let me just say that what I think we should do is. . ."

Now when anyone says, "What we should do," it is almost always followed by the realization that this is really something *I* should do. I pulled away and gave her a glare. I was starting to have some real resentment here. I felt like I did when I was ugly skinny M in high school, with all the mean girls mocking me. Only now I was ugly fat-saggy stomach M.

Being the great saleswoman that she was, Marianne caught on immediately and lifted a pale perfect hand in protest, as she assured me, "No, no darling, do not be concerned. I just think that you're coming here is so brave, so *forward*. Let's get the most from this visit, shall we?" I assumed she was discreetly referring to the $150 consultation fee—and that I'd want to get my "money's worth."

Well, when you put it like that...

After a forty-five-minute consultation, I drove home in shock. I not only needed a liposuction, but a tummy-tuck, a face lift and an eyelift. Why did they charge separately? Aren't the eyes part of the face? Marianne also "strongly" suggested that I get a neck lift and laser treatment to reduce my large cavernous pores and any leftover wrinkles that were not stretched and tucked into the top of my head. Total cost of my makeover? Well, first let me tell you that no doctor ever discusses the money part of this procedure. That little dirty job duty is assigned to a behind the scenes "billing department."

I was escorted to a luxuriously appointed office, also decorated in shades of lavender. Marianne gestured, "Lorie Anne vill assist you with your–" She made an attempt to grimace, "financial concerns." Then the doctor vanished.

Lorie Anne, the "the Bill-gal," looked as if she has had every type of cosmetic surgery known to womankind. She of course, was the requisite size two, five foot six, with pin-straight long blonde hair, size D boobs, and her perfect size six feet were ensconced in four-inch high Christian Louboutin heels. She directed me to sit down, then placed a blue bottle of high-end water in front of me. I'd no doubt that I needed the water to ward off the panic attack as she began perusing a paper that Marianne had handed her.

"Let's see, a number 42A–that's going to be an *estimate* of fifteen thousand."

"What's a '42A' and why is it going to cost fifteen thousand dollars? And why an *estimate*?" I croaked as I gripped the lip of the water bottle, twisting it violently.

"Oh, well, that's your *simple* face lift and it will *probably* cost fifteen thousand–unless the Doctor encounters any problems."

I'm rocked forward in complete horror and I rasped, "What kind of encounters would jack up the price of my facelift?" By this time, I had started shaking. Problems? *Like I know that people have died having this done…. Shit.*

Gal-person demurred, "well, just because. I mean, it's a simple facelift, but it could get *complex…*"

She paused and gave me an intense look that communicated clearly that if I'd just look in the mirror, I'd get why it was a fifteen-thousand-dollars plus repair job. She did that thing–that damn double-eye-roll-toss-my-blonde-hair-in-exasperation gesture and raised her perfect brows, "Now, may I continue?" She glanced down at her Cartier watch, letting me know that I was interfering with her lunch when she would get to eat three peas and a carrot stick.

I nodded, "By all means, pick away at my life's savings."

She ignored my ironic sense of humor and indeed, ticked away: "Eyelift, forty-five hundred and then a 15R–oh, I see," I noticed that she was speaking in "hundreds" as it seems less painful than thousands.

She gave me a knowing look at my droopy chest and flashed her recently bleached teeth, "Doctor did mention that need for breast implants?"

I looked down at my chest—straight down to my lumpy thighs—no barrier. "I really don't think I need… that is, it's not in my budget–"

She interrupted me, "Well, Doctor is not going to really *charge* you, but let's see, there will be a nine-hundred-dollar fee any way for any 1011R–"

"Oh! Oh!" I raised my hand like a kindergartener, "Let me guess: that's the code for the anesthesiologist, right?" *And, is a fee less than a charge?* I thought I was being funny, but Gal straightened me out right quick.

Bill-Gal shook her head in disappointment, "No, actually that means the actual anesthesia."

I paled. "Anesthesia? But doesn't the drug come with the doctor? Like a package deal or something?

She blinked at me. "Do you want to skip the *full* anesthesia?" She gave me a long-lash fierce stare, "we do offer a semi-awake mode." She glanced at my not fashionable purse, practically boring a hole to my wallet and added, "it saves money and some people enjoy watching the procedure."

Semi-awake? Is that legal? Enjoy watching? Is she shitting me? I dropped my wobbly chin to my sagging neck.

I imagined Husband and accounting columns. If he were here, no doubt he'd be going for cost-reduction options. Well, I decided that if my husband even *entertained* such a money-saving concept for a second, I would grab a scalpel and slice *him* to shreds.

I gave Bill-gal a scowl, hopefully the last one I'd be able to do once my forehead was tied behind my ponytail and hissed, "No.

I do not want to watch the surgery. No thank you."

Blonde hair flicked back from the perfectly sculpted face and Bill-gal exhaled, "All right then, are you ready for more information?"

"More fees you mean," I hissed under my breath.

When she got done, my "spackling job" was going to cost me over forty grand. I could save money if I put a stick in my mouth and avoided being put out, or if I chose to forgo the use of a surgeon during the procedure. Other than that, my savings were to be screwed.

Forty thousand dollars! I thought about my teaching retirement savings. I was supposed to use that someday to live on, but what was the point if I hated the way I looked and lived? I tried to imagine a cute low-slung BMW convertible that I could buy with that money. Then I visualized my saggy face being pushed backwards by the wind on the freeway. I knew that Husband was not going to approve. Shit, he might even try to forbid. I took a breath and made myself ready for battle.

That night I plied him with wine and hinted at sex. After a long debate during which he insisted that I was "gorgeous" just as I am, and me sobbing into my hands, occasionally tugging on my jowls for effect, he at least agreed to join me back at Dr. Fix-it's office for a "spousal consultation." I think he was motivated by the promise that the doctor took off the one-hundred-fif-ty-dollar consultation fee if one had the surgery. Oh, and we had sex that night.

Marianne was of the philosophy that one healed much bet-ter when one's spouse was gung-ho about the surgery. I think it was more along the lines of One Gets Paid If One Husband Buys into the Pitch. Husband and I sat in the examination room. He, in his usual sweatshirt and jeans, me, in my fabulous mauve dressing gown.

When the doc came in, my husband who previously had claimed that he "didn't like blondes" nearly keeled over when the five foot eight, perfect Dr. Fix-it extended her hand. She was wearing a fantastic lavender clingy creation that coordinated beautifully with the surrounding uterine-pink walls and my dressing gown. She must have had every hair on her body removed, because there were no visible fuzz, lumps, bumps, or mounds of any kind other than those goddess breasts and her pert little bottom. She lowered her black lashes over her today-violet hued eyes, tossed her platinum blonde waves and purred, "Hello, I am so pleased to see *you* here."

She kept eye contact with my spouse. Apparently, he was her target. I was just peripheral clutter. Husband offered her a fish-limp handshake and then melted into a nearby chair. I was surprised his butt made it into the chair, since his eyes were glued to her chest.

I sat silent, trying figure out if her eyes were really purple or alien green—or just plain brown like most of us earthlings.

She reached up on the door hook and put on a lavender stylishly fitted smock. Now that she was dressed for the hunt, she shared her strategic plan to overhaul Husband's wife. As Marianne spoke, the accent kept thickening. Every time she'd mentioned one of my malformed body parts and planned rehabilitation, Husband would frown.

Five minutes into her presentation, my husband looked as if *he* might need his own Botox. Then Dr. Fix-it pulled one on me. First, she asked me to step out of the gown. I started to protest and she glared at me with a laser purple stare. Cowed, I stood, naked and completely humiliated. I don't know why I felt so naked, but I was after all *naked*. Yes, there was my husband, but somehow it all seemed so weird to have Dr. Fix-it as an audience and *critic*. I looked longingly at the crumbled lavender pile on the chaise. Dr. Fix-it continued rattling off what was needed to "pep up" my body and face. She reached inside the pocket of her designer-gown-not-even-close-to-being-a-smock, and extracted a gold Mont Blanc pen. Her pen jabbed my thighs, then she drew an ink map on my neck and my jowls.

I kept takin deep breaths, but I was rattled. My blood pressured soared when she poked the pen under my left droopy-boob, lifting the lifeless thing up. She pulled the pen out and shook her head with pity as my titty oozed down over my ribs. Turning her back on me and cleverly directing her words to my husband, she announced, "You know vhat? I'm going to throw in a boob job for just two thousand dollars more. It's my gift to *you*." She batted her eyes at my man.

"What?" I gasped, completely taken aback. *And money numbers had drifted out of her puffy lips!*

Surely, he'd agree that I didn't need a boob-job. *He loved my breasts.* He said so just last night. Ready for Husband's shared indignation, I whipped my head around just in time to catch the bastard exhaling, "Wow. Ah. . . that would be. . . Great?"

Dr. Fix-it beamed, shrugged her shoulders, adding, "You know, that is actually free. The money only covers the anesthesiologist's extra time and of course, the implants."

Outraged, I protested, "But my husband loves my–"

Husband-pig, interrupted me with, "How big?"

I whirled around and growled, "What?"

"Darlings!" The accent disappeared. This was business time. She actually snapped her fingers at me, demanding my attention.

She leaned towards me, waving her golden pen at me and demanded, "Look,"

I cringed as she took her pen and started poking again at my breasts.

I gave a weak, half-assed protest, "Please, stop that?"

"You see," she glanced behind me and sideways. Now she wasn't even talking to me, but directing her attention to The Wallet.

"These," poke, poke, "are damaged. They are…well, *empty.*"

Empty? Like a milk carton? No, more like those juice packets that I used to give the kids. I looked down at my boobs. Tentatively, I pushed at the spongy stuff that was once a perky 34B. Oh-my-god, they *did* look like little empty sacks… with walnuts! I looked across at my husband, who was staring at me as if these were not the boobs he knew and loved.

He looked just a tiny bit contrite. That lasted around five seconds, before he gestured towards my little flaps and mouthed silently, "poor things."

Poor things? I stared at my boobs, then at the doctor, then my husband, then back to my barely size B's, lying limply along the top of my floppy stomach. I felt resentment bubbling up my saggy tummy. What happened to the "love for better or worse" promise? I glared over and then down to the pouf around the top of my husband's not-so-small-belly. Not as if *he* was perfect. Yet, I rationalized, in all fairness, this whole make over thing was my idea. I closed my slightly puffy-saggy eyes and tried to picture myself as a size C with a tight tummy and a new face. My high school reunion was that summer. I remembered the tenth reunion, seeing my classmates, both friend and foe, like Mean Judy Blakely, Prom Queen and Bitch.

I exhaled in defeat to the harsh reality: I needed some work done and I needed it soon, before the entire structure collapsed and there was anything to glue on to. I relented, "Well, if you think I need it. . . OK."

All of a sudden, the hubby perked right up. In fact, the little pervert was so thrilled that he was getting a new pair of boobs to play with, that he offered to pay for the entire makeover. The craziest part is that he agreed to get an eyelift himself after I healed. Yes, Marianne was that good of a saleswoman.

He needn't have delayed; there was no way I was going to depend on him as my nurse. I wisely booked my sister for the special event–well, at least I *thought* asking my sister was a good idea. The "special event" is about putting yourself into a horror movie as both the monster and the victim.

Of course, I knew it wasn't going to be a picnic. But I figured a few days of extreme discomfort, some bruising and then, at the next parent meeting–the new me. Problem was that the new me still had an old me inside and *that* was a slow healer and a wimp! By the second day of recovery, which was in fact, not a recovery, but just the second day of more-agony-than-Vicodin-can conquer, I was convinced that I had made a very big mistake. Unlike the women on TV who have the extreme makeovers, I wasn't in any swanky recovery facility. I was home. Home with Thing One and Thing Two, my husband and my sister, who I can only describe as a humanoid form of a hamster.

All of them were making me crazy. Thing Two started crying every time she saw me, sobbing accusingly, "Why did you have to do this? You were fine. Now you are really scary and are you going to look like this when you drive me for my field trip to the Art Museum next week?"

"Oomph," I was only able to make guttural non-word sounds in response. I tried to scribble on a pad of paper, "No, because I am not going to the damn museum, your Aunty Flora is going to take you."

Thing Two had read the note, crumbled it up and jammed it into her jeans pocket and huffed, "Oh great! Now I get dorky Aunty Flora leading our group. Mom, you know that she is like a camp leader."

Thing One decided to chime in, "Yeah, a camp leader-on-crack! Jeez Mom, way to go. Thing Two will be in therapy for years over this. What about all those self-esteem issues you're always reading to me about—that we need to treasure our *inner* beauty. Crap."

"Agh, fin' whn' you r twenty." I was attempting to garble, *Natural inner beauty–Fine when you're twenty.*

The eldest sneered, taking advantage of the fact that I was immobile, "Huh? What are you saying, Mom? That you're a hypocrite?"

"Oomph!" translated to *Fuck You People*.

I made another unintelligible sound, which Thing One understood to mean, "And where is your aunt anyway?"

"She went to get her toes done."

Great, some nurse. I tried to rise out of the recliner, but stopped myself and winced. I could feel one of the staples in my head tugging on my stretched-out scalp. I sighed with self-pity and admitted that my sister probably needed a break from the Family.

She had been doing night duty for five nights, and that was no picnic. Then there's the day time care-taking duties of dragging my bandaged ass to the restroom, hosing me down in the shower while I was fully encased in a sausage-like rubber garment that was compressing my newly sculpted belly and hips into a Madonna-like shape. And had to come up with creative ways to turn every kind of food into gruel. I really kept her hopping all night, because I kept limping from room to room, convinced that somewhere in my house was a surface that I could *recline* on, (one must keep one's head up after a facelift so that it stays a *FACE LIFT*), and not make me scream in pain. Every time I shuffled from my bed, to the den, to the family room, to the living room, my poor sister would trail behind me, her barf pail in one hand, and a bag of ice in the other.

I know that I was a lousy patient, but it was really hard to be cooperative when even your husband is acting horrified every time he walked by. For example, on the third day of my attempt at "recovery," he passed me with his face all scrunched up croaked, "Jeez honey, you look like Sonny Liston after he lost a fight."

I responded with whimpering sounds and a narrowing of my very puffy eyelids.

"Oh no, M, M, don't cry, I see that you look like you're hurting."

"Oomph, oomph. Oomph!"

My sister returned from the nail salon, with lovely pink toes and French manicure. She did a great job making dinner and even commandeered the kids into cleaning up the kitchen, because she totally terrified them. The phone had been ringing like crazy. I had been of course, drugged and clueless. Prior to the surgery, we had a family meeting (I know Flora was there, although she later denied it.) No one in the neighborhood was to know about my "project." After all, it wasn't anyone's business. The story was that I'd just "be out of town," my sister filling in and I'd return, say in two weeks, (Okay, I now knew, more like three or four weeks,) later simply "refreshed and rested." That plan apparently went kaput as soon as my sister first answered the phone.

"M? Oh yes, well, she's resting. Oh...well, yes, she *was* out of town, but... Oh no! She's not *sick*. No, she had a facelift. And liposuction!" As if she suddenly realizes that she wasn't supposed to say anything, she could be heard whispering the coupe de gras, "and a boob job."

The "cat" was way out of the bag and it unleashed a flurry of sly kitties who immediately were at my door, camouflaged with dinners, flowers, cookies, just "looking in on M" when we all knew they were here to see the sideshow freak. And I sure didn't disappoint them. I kept getting more and more swollen, bluer, with tinges of green and a speckle of yellow. I never knew that I had so many "concerned neighbors."

Meow.

One such feline couldn't even pretend to actually care about me; she brought a digital camera. When I threw my hands up in the air to shield my poor bandaged face, she shrieked, "but M, I want to document this for the Book Club! Le'me see those boobs!"

"Oomph!" I summoned up all my vocal abilities and screeched, "Are you fucking crazy? Get out of my house!"

She unfortunately didn't understand pain-bandage talk and remained in my living room. Mercifully, Thing One took her camera away telling her that she was a tactless bitch and that her mother would get even and wear a cocktail dress cut down to her newly-placed navel at her next dinner party. That shooed her out. God bless that kid of mine.

Then there was the Big Surprise. Apparently, my husband must have slipped Dr. Fix-it some extra cash, because I didn't get 34C's, but 34D's. I kept wondering why all the other swelling was going down, but not my boobs. When I accused him of violating my body intactness, he claimed that Dr. Fix-it had consulted with me just before the surgery and had determined that I'd look more "balanced" with larger breasts *and* he swore, I had agreed with her and signed an addendum document.

"What was it called—the *'I want a wife with really big titties' document?'*" I glared at Husband for clarification.

He replied lowly, "Well, you know…your…uh… hips and butt aren't getting any work done and…well…you will look more *balanced*." Then he fled the room. I vaguely recalled the doctor chatting with me while I floated in pre-surgery Nirvana high of Valium about "balance." Well, we'd have to see. If it looked really bad, I could always start making porn movies. I'd really opened Pandora's box with that man of mine…

Getting completely over-hauled is like a little death of one's old self and just like any loss, there is a kind of Grief that occurs. Yes, there is a "re-birth," but it's not just all about going to the lingerie store and buying your first 34D bra–it's a process.

Step One: **Excruciating Pain**. Pain so bad that you question your sanity for embarking on such a stupid idea. You have staples in your head, drains in your neck that were very gross, a gigantic ace bandage around your head for four nights, a bra made of latex and steel, and that lovely girdle compressing your bruised innards.

Step Two: **More Pain, followed by Depression**. It's over, I survived anesthesia, why am I so sad? Could it be because I am continually stooped over from the tummy tuck stitches? Or the fact that my thighs seem to be on a never-ending quest to retain water so that I'm swelling to *twice* the size I was *before* the surgery? Or just that I look really, really ugly?

Step Three: **Continual Pain and…Doubt.** What if my face is stretched so tight that I look like Aunt Tessie at my Bat Mitzvah? Will my safety belt fit over the new boobs? Will I have to reset the controls on my seat in the car? What if my they feel so hard that it turns off my husband or what if I injure someone if I bump into him? Or even worse, what if they feel so good that he (the Husband) won't leave me alone?

Step Four: **Embarrassment/Denial**. "*Me*, a facelift? Oh, don't be ridiculous. I just went to the spa, lost some weight, and started spin class. I look fifteen years younger? Oh phsaw, you're so sweet! But no, just face cream and a glass of wine every night." Followed by an attempt to smirk, but the stitches on my head still pull.

Step Five: **Withholding.** *I have a secret.* My skin is wrinkle free because my cheeks are stapled to the top of my head and my scalp has been numb for six weeks. I'm bent over double not because I have pre-menopausal cramping, but because my stomach muscles are now attached to my ass! I currently am wearing the same kind of blouses I did when I was nursing because my boobs are four times their normal size. Not that I *know* what my new "normal" is.

So, recovery was slow. For some reason, I was retaining water and my thighs, so recently sucked fatless, looked huge. I couldn't wear jeans. I couldn't wear leggings, only my *husband's* sweat pants. Not good.

Dr. Fix-it's Nazi receptionist was completely unsympathetic. She offered me a referral to a specialist who dealt with toxins. Great, the toxic receptionist gave me a referral to a toxin remover? I made an appointment because I was really getting worried about the swelling. I looked like the Michelin man, err, woman, with huge boobs.

The no-toxics treatment spa was called "Shake it Away." I arrived early to the cutely decorated baby pink salon.

"Mercedes," yes, she was an optimistic girl, greeted me in her yoga pants, crop top and flat tummy.

"Oh, you look great.... but toxic, right? I'm scheduling liposuction myself." The bitch patted her concave stomach and batted her two-inch eyelashes, "I'm just *so* fat! Do you like your surgeon?"

How was I supposed to answer this twit? *Yes, I'm bloated full of something. No, my doctor was weird, and greedy, and how dare you complain about your under twenty-one-year-old body?* Instead I just shrugged my shoulders as high as my ten pound breasts would allow.

She gestured for me to stand on a pedestal (at last!!) and she began to wrap my chunky thighs with wet gauze.

"This is essence of tea tree oil. It absorbs toxins."

"Uh, huh?" I looked down at her as she circled my body.

"Then you're going to dance for one hour."

"What?" Had she been smoking the tea tree?

She stood up, hands on non-existent hips and she nodded, "Yup, well, you can stomp, jump, swing, or whatever—just need to keep moving."

Apparently, I had lost all vocabulary: "Huh?"

"For one hour."

"Wha'?"

She dropped her heavy lashes, sighed in a pleasant, exasperated tone, "Oh, didn't they explain it to you? You have to keep moving for the toxins to move out. Oh, and be prepared–you're going to pee a *lot!*"

Great, peeing was a major challenge. The mandatory post-op-girdle I had worn had a "hole" in it, to allegedly pee through.

Only a sniper marksman could ever shoot through that thing, so I had to unpeel myself from the spandex/elastic shroud and nearly launch out of the restroom, not to mention, that I had to lie down prone to yank it back on. *Ugh.*

Mercedes stood back, pulled a curtain that was somewhat like a hospital privacy barrier and I was in my own little tent of pink. Then she drifted to a music docking station. "Do you want hip-hop, rap, classic rock or pop?"

"Huh?" I was still quite speechless. I was going to *dance?* For a *fucking hour?*

When I didn't answer, she took matters into her own hands and put on a R&B disk. "Most people like this the best; it really motivates you to move."

I was motivated to move all right, to run right out the door. However, I was currently in my super-girdle and twenty feet of wet ace bandage. So, what-the-hell, I was in for a penny, in for a pound...err...bloat.

I danced. For one hour. I peed for four. I looked better. Why, I don't really know if it worked, but...

I also, having invested so much in my face and body, did keep up the good work going to the gym, slathering myself with sunscreen, and spackling, and injecting the new face every six months with Botox and fillers. I've made way too much of an investment to let this stuff drop.

Although I don't think that I am capable of ever going through the discomfort of surgery again, I have got to admit that around two months later, I looked, well, as Thing One would say, "Stoked. Hot."

Meow.

I did go to that tactless neighbor's dinner party and I attempted to flirt with her dumpy husband, as I chanted under my breath, "Don't you wish your *wife* was hot like me, don't cha?"

It was fantastic going to my high school reunion looking like I just got out of high school (well kind of.) Then there were fringe benefits as well. My newly reconstructed body needed new clothes.

Oh, and big surprise, the hubby really *did* love the new boobs. He showed the love by buying lots of sexy underwear assembles from numerous catalogues. Some of them were ridiculous, but after all, it is about *man-woman* love too, right?

CHAPTER NINE

Two Days and Forty-Five Minutes with Vanna White

IT ALL STARTED WHEN THING ONE WAS SURFING THE Internet. "Why are you playing around with the Net—don't you have homework?"

"Moth-er, I'm taking a break. Come here. Look. I just entered our names in the Wheel of Fortune Mothers' Day special contest! If I win the drawing, we'd qualify for an application, and then they screen the applications, and then if we pass *that,* we go for an interview, and then another one and then *we could be on the show!*" She took a breath and looked up at her lost-for-words-mom.

Well, that sounded far-fetched enough for me, I was distracted with paying bills, trying to figure out if we could still send her to college if we just ate beans for four years... So, I just nodded sweetly and said, "That's nice honey. Good job. Now do your homework." *Bless the youth and their optimism.*

I figured that it was like entering a sweepstakes or winning the lottery–*fat chance.*

I was wrong. After my eldest child filled out a questionnaire that was as deeply probing as any college application, she received a confirming email. Could she and her dumb-struck mother please report in to the *to-be-disclosed-upon-agreement-building* on January 5th at precisely 10:00 a.m.?

I couldn't believe it. I also couldn't admit that I barely ever watched Wheel of Fortune. I'd glanced over at it while preparing dinner, while my crazy kid who is a word-master did–every night. Over the years, besides winning every spelling bee she'd ever entered always demonstrating the uncanny ability to spell any word backwards that proved to be highly entertaining at Bar Mitzvahs and weddings. She was an avid crossword puzzler. She did *not* get this talent from her unable-to-spell-anything-without-spell-check Mother.

So, we reported in for what I thought was just an interview. Before we did, my daughter went over our wardrobe and forced me to buy two gag-me pink sweater sets. I still can't believe that either one of us would be caught dead in a *sweater set*. However, she had read that pink was very *flattering, soft and appealing* and she was sure they'd be video recording us to see if we were photogenic. Reluctantly, I spent two-hundred dollars on two sets of sweaters that I pretty much knew would never be worn again.

We took a taxi because she stated brutally that she did not trust my driving or parking karma to get us there on time. Thing One clutched the directions against her chest. We arrived twenty minutes early at a building somewhere downtown, where, if we ended up kidnap victims, I'd never be able to describe to the cops. We saw no one. Thing One banged on the rust colored metal door.

"Are you sure this was the address?" I looked around for perverts and murders.

"Oh Mom, lighten up. Yes. We're early that's all." *Early? How is it possible that I've spent most of my time mothering nagging this child to wake up for school?*

She continued banging until a tall formidable security guard opened the door.

"You ladies are early." He glared down at me, the obvious culprit for arriving too early.

"We wanted to make sure we'd be on time." I straightened my pink shoulders and glared up at him.

"Well, Mama, I can't let you ladies in until check in time." He nodded at me, clearly convinced that I was indeed "the too early problem."

Thing one batted her lashes and whimpered, "but it's cold out here."

The guard looked us up and down, shook his head. "You've both got on…those *pink* sweaters." He smirked.

I flushed. *Damn, sweater sets.*

Thing One relented until she wore him down. Finally, he checked our photo ID's, scanned our letter of acceptance twice, and waved us inside. We shuffled into a small room, cramped with folding chairs. The room was *really* freezing; I clung to my cardigan sweater. Within five minutes there were fifty pairs of moms/young adult kids stuffed in the room.

Two producers arrived looking like they were about my daughter's age. One, a woman, who talked so fast that I found myself squinting, my head tilted sideways like a dog, struggling to understand her. In rapid fire, she shot out an overview of what the program's producers were looking for as contestants for the show. Basically, you had to act as if you were not just *high* on life, but on *crack*. We were to jump up and down, squeal with enthusiasm, but cut it off as soon as Pat Sajak spoke or Vanna White drifted near.

We then played a mock game of Wheel. Thing One and I were ridiculously high-on-life. We jumped, squealed, giggled and shut up on command. Cameras rolled and we acted nonchalant. We were perky and adorable in our matching pink sweaters.

Following a modest lunch of flat sandwiches with something beige that might have been chicken, alongside a tiny apple and a Barbie doll bag of potato chips (that I assumed was more than Vanna was allowed to eat,) we were escorted into a vast room with rows of school desks. Once we were seated, we were told that we would have a "few" little tests to take. They then passed around four pages of word puzzles and three # 2 pencils per person. I thumbed through the material and at first didn't take it too seriously. *After all, how hard could this be?*

I failed most of them miserably. Clearly, I should have watched the show. And maybe studied the dictionary. Multiple #2 pencils should have been a warning sign. Twenty minutes before I was even done trudging through a three-paragraph word puzzle, my daughter gleefully announced that she had finished every one of them and wasn't that fun?

I hung my head in shame and apologized for the fact that we would not be chosen for the show because her mother was a moron and had barely answered five out of the fifty questions.

Ever the optimist, she replied,

"Oh no, that's good–because they don't want you too smart– then you'd be a ringer. So not getting them right might be just the right strategy. Good call Mom!" *Oh, good grief, I thought, she thinks I acted stupid on purpose?* I was so hungry for approval from my teenage daughter that I just zipped it. Why did she need the truth anyway?

All those years of my encouraging her for her brightness, her achievements, and she was proud of me for my spelling disability.

Two weeks later, we got a notice. "Congratulations: **you** are even closer to be on **Wheel-of-Fortune!**" If we made this next cut, we would be taping for the Mother's Day Special.

I dropped my book club selection, all fashion magazines and started doing crossword puzzles and leafing through the Thesaurus. I watched with my daughter, Wheel every night. One week after the letter, we got "secure" directions. On our way, I was going frantically through my contacts list, trying to think of every friend and family member I had. We were going to need back-up screeching and applause—but that was of course, if we made this final audition. Of course, Thing One had no doubt. She'd already sent out a "heads-up" email to all her friends.

We arrived not at a studio, but at the Moscone Convention Center. We were half awake, clad in our matching sweaters. It was seven-thirty in the morning. I had already chuckled about the fact that Thing One never got up early without a violent shaking every morning, but here were—on time—*again*.

We were herded into a room and divided up. More mock performances. Then we were culled out once again. I was shocked when I realized that we made the final cut. I'm sure it was those sweater sets. Yes, you can see it on the tape of the show. We *softly* stood out in our pink.

We witnessed the producers and their assistants snapping their fingers at the contestants while ranting, "Come on! Juice it up! Jump! Clap! Be happy!". We were visited by Pat. He is a nice man with a kind of large head–not conceited, his head is really large. Guess you need a big head for a large brain to remember all those peoples' names and backgrounds. Vanna also had come to visit. She was encased in a fluffy white bathrobe that swallowed her pencil thin body. I wanted to hate her: sans makeup she is still gorgeous and very sweet.

I wondered if she liked having to wear all those silly evening gowns in the middle of the morning; suffocating from the spews of hairspray and spray tan? She seemed so calm as she spoke to us with a whisper of a voice, gentle and modulated. I have no idea what she said to us, but I fell in love with her immediately.

Vanna left, and people came in pushing rolling carts. We were given a light snack (burping is not acceptable behavior while taping.) We were told to brush our teeth before reporting into the make-up room. They handed out mini toothbrushes and paste to those of us who didn't read our "extensive instructions regarding hygiene." Thing One and I pushed our mini granola bar around and shook our heads, rejecting it at last. I prayed that my stomach didn't start rumbling in high definition stereo on stage.

After we brushed our teeth, our keepers herded the group into a harshly lit room and introduced the makeup artists. We were each assigned our own makeup person, aka, *Wizard*. Mine looked at me, frowned, then and lied, "Why, you are absolutely gorgeous! I don't think I'll have to do anything but dab a little lipstick on you." I looked around at my cohorts—everyone was getting some makeup. My self-esteem fell right through my fuzzy pink sweater. Maybe she felt that I too homely to even attempt to repair? You know the old saying, "Oh, I don't photograph well"? Bull Shit. *You're just ugly.* After all, this was before my Dr. Fix-it experience.

"I get kind of washed out in pink." I offered lamely.

The Wizard gave me a critical eye. "Hmm… right, yes." She then spackled me right over. At the last minute, she glued on false lashes. I went from not-needing-anything, to a full make-over.

"The eyes are so distracting—from any flaws. Err… not that you have any…flaws."

I wisely didn't respond. It was rather difficult to blink.

After makeup, we were escorted to the set. Standing behind the stage, the producers reminded us that they'd be shouting at us to be "energetic" in-between taping. This translated into a litany that went something like this:

"Hey-you! Pick and Push! Pick and Push!" I had no idea what-in-the-hell they were talking about until Thing One explained, "Pick a letter quickly Mom and 'push' it out of your mouth, like you're crazy excited!"

Uh huh.

Before the taping began the assistant directors reviewed our prize opportunities. We were told that the dollar grand prize was "sizeable." Indeed, they were: prizes: a SUV kind of wagon and a sports car. Besides the money, the winning Mother/son or Mother/daughter pair would *each* get a car. We were told to decide who got what now and upon cue (and winning), we were to run to *our* car, signal our family-in-the-audience up on the stage, and gleefully, with demonstrative gratitude, pile into said vehicles.

Thing one and I began arguing immediately. I already had a damn SUV and I wanted the cute sexy sports car. Besides, I reasoned, she had always wanted to drive *my* van and she'd murdered it. Pat timed us out. No joke. He had us sit on the bottom stage steps and "work out our strategy."

"It's not fair Mom, *I* got us on this show."

I nodded in agreement, flipped my two-inch long lashes and added, "It's *Mother's Day* show. Without me, there is no *mother*." At last, Thing One relented, relinquishing the sporty car to her deserving mother.

That done, we toddled over to the stage. It was blistering hot with lights. I was pre-menopausal-sweating-in-my-pink-sweater set. The Wheel was gigantic and Thing One and I were short. We had figured that since we'd be standing for a while, we should wear sensible shoes. That was fine, except we were *short*. They had elevator pillars that we stood on, only once they were high enough for the audience to see us, she and I could barely reach down to spin the wheel. We did some practice spins and let me tell you, that sucker is heavy and cumbersome. That game is not for sissies.

Red lights flashed and the curtain opened. I nearly threw up. The entire auditorium was filled. I recalled that the each of convention halls had about a hundred and fifty thousand square feet, and all that was visible of the audience darkness was a sea of faces. I took a breath and did a yoga exhale (finally, that class paid off,) and smiled a big toothy enthusiastic *I'm-wearing-dumb-pink and I'm proud of it* smile. I batted my heavy-duty lashes and blinked into the lights.

We won the first round, that is my *daughter* won. She cleverly solved the first word puzzle with, "Choosy mothers chose Jif!" It was all downhill from there. We were out-maneuvered by an older gal who clearly watched Wheel of Fortune twenty-four-seven. I assumed that her pseudo "I'm-just-a-construction-worker-son," was actually a *Harvard graduate*, who had majored in linguistics. They creamed us. Thing One and I did not win the Grand Prize or The SUV or The Sports Car, but we did get one thousand dollars for *Jif Peanut Butter* guess. We had a good time, not to mention the mother-daughter bonding experience.

So what did it matter that we never wore our matching Mother/Daughter dorky pink sweater sets again? The tape came in handy when we wanted to set up a bet, "Bet cha' didn't know that my mom and I were on TV?" We'd roll the tape and watch with pride as everyone gasped with surprise.

We were celebrities. Since it was on video, we could stretch our fame out over the years. Neat.

We ignored the comments: "M., I never knew you wore *pink*. Wow, your lashes are so long and *thick*. Thing One, you were so happy and *chatty*. It's great to not see you being a sullen teenager, ha, ha—just kidding."

The inevitable question as to why we didn't do better was kindly deferred by my daughter as "well, it was really *hard* to spin that wheel." She filled me with pride and affection when she took the words right out of my mouth as she disclaimed,

"Hey, it's not about the winning, it was about the love."

CHAPTER TEN

My Carpool Days Are Over, but I Keep Spinning My Wheels

WHEN THE LAST KID LEFT FOR COLLEGE I DECIDED TO START *really* enjoying myself. Due to double college tuitions, enjoying myself did not include traveling yet. I did insist that Husband and I start going out at least once a week, as in a *real* date night; movie and dinner.

"But you make such great dinners at home," he offered weakly.

"Not the point babe. We need to get out of the house."

"But now that the girls are gone, we can actually *eat* dinner and there's no arguments or whining or texting."

That was true. However, after three months of quiet dinner time, where he fled to watch television while I, supposedly grateful for no helpers to nag, cleaned up the kitchen, I decided that we needed to upgrade our lifestyle—or get a live-in cook.

Husband countered, "Well, I can cook two or three times a week."

"Eating Bar-B-Q that often is feeding a precancerous stomach lining. No, I want us to go out."

"Aren't you going to go out with your girlfriends?"

"Yup. And *you* are going out with me. You can have a night out with the boys, or a Saturday to golf, or–"

"M., I don't golf and I really don't have a lot of men friends. I like to be home, and just, well, veg."

"Oh, don't I know."

He finally agreed that it was a good idea. It would be like when we first got married, with no kids, and again, not much money. Of course, this took some negotiation. Sex was now included in the date night package.

Because our social life was set with the hubby, I decided to expand my intellect by starting a book club. My ad placed on the Internet asked that only woman over *fifty*, whose kiddies were out of the house or at least beyond elementary school, have a sense of humor and actually like to read, need apply. I received twelve responses. Two were men who thought they looked like women-over-fifty. They were expelled because they were not the right gender and one of them looked better than I did in a dress. Three were housewives with toddlers who tried to withhold the information until someone let it slip that she had to get home before the babysitter charged her double. We patted her on the back and told her that for her own safety she didn't want to hang around some cranky menopausal women who'd come to resent their husbands, resent their children and whose veins ran deep with Botox. All three young ladies wisely fled for their lives.

There were seven ladies left including me–all of us over fifty and allegedly, *mature*. However, I had settled too soon, as we began to have internal issues that threaten the stability of our little self-education entity. The newest member, was a lawyer for the IRS. We figured out that she had a major drinking problem when she arrived completely "sauced up" to every meeting, didn't read the book.

She spent the evening belligerently ranting about "stupid ninnies and bitches." We weren't quite sure if we were looped into the former or latter category. She ranted on that some women "had nothing better to do than read." When she was to be a guest at a hostess's home, she arrived late, by taxi thank goodness, stumbled around and sat away from the group, mumbling.

On more than one occasion, I reminded her that this was indeed, a *book* club, hence reading was encouraged.

She snarled back at me, "I'm a damn lawyer! You think I have a lot of time for pleasure reading this crap? I just wanted a little release from all the citizens trying to rob the U.S. government."

We all looked around sheepishly, trying to recall if we had any suspicious deductions she might turn up.

When it was her turn to host, I went with a lot of angst. I walked to the front of her building. There was more security than at a government office. A video camera twirled above my head, and then with technological creepiness, goose-necked until it was face to face with me. Cautiously, I punched in her apartment number.

A raspy voice crackled over the speaker. "Who-the-hell is it?"

"Err… it's M, from book club. You're hosting tonight?"

No response, but the door suddenly buzzed. After an up and down ride on the elevator, I figured out that she was in the penthouse.

The door was ajar. I looked around hopefully for other members, or at least the hostess. The dark entryway was empty. There was a small round table with bottles of hard liquor and tumblers.

"Hel-lo?"

A muffled voice barked, "Just have a seat. I'll be out in a minute."

I meandered into the living room. A couch, two chairs, coffee table, no humans. No food in sight. My stomach rumbled. The lawyer-hostess appeared from the darkness.

"What do you want to drink?"

"Err… do you have wine?"

"Are you shitting me? No, I have *real* alcohol."

Well, what-the-hell, I'd probably need a stiff one to survive this night.

"Scotch, neat."

"That a girl!" She smiled for the first time in two months.

When the doorbell rang, I sighed in relief. I wasn't alone with her. The other ladies drifted in. Everyone was starving, but there were only martini olives to munch on. We had eight members, but only four seats. When I meandered to the dining room to fetch extra chairs, the lawyer barked, "No—*not* those. They stay there."

I nodded mutely. Four of us took turns sitting on the floor. We rotated so that no one got completely crippled. Once we were all seated, numb from the hard floor, lack of food, and strong booze, the lawyer announced that she hadn't read the book—the one *she* had selected. Seemed a good indication that she wasn't going to fit in. We exchanged glances, silently communicating. *How do we get out of here gracefully?*

Why were we worrying about manners, I had no idea. Being ladies of the book club, we endured a wretched evening, and slightly buzzed, we left her home and met at the local diner to eat dinner and figure an escape plan.

One of our members, a soft-spoken social worker, exhaled, "I mean, I don't want to get her angry—she works for the IRS for godsakes!"

Another wisely noted, "Can't get her much angrier; I say we just send her a letter that we've dissolved the book club due to lack of interest."

"Yeah, *her* lack of interest!"

We nodded in agreement and stuffed our faces with pie. Pie, is always a good cure for too much imbibing. As it was, she saved us the effort. After the meeting, she sent an email indicating that based on the books we selected (Pulitzer prize winners of course,) that we were clearly morons and she could no longer (after two meetings) suffer fools.

Thank God.

We settled into what we hoped to be at last, peaceful exploration of literature. Everyone interacted very nicely. Two single moms had formed a close friendship. We noticed that they were carpooling together and apparently exchanging family dinners. They shared the book, brought appetizers together.

One evening, sitting in a hostess's living room, we waited patiently for the two missing ladies to arrive. No show and then suddenly I got a text message.

Let me just preface this with the reminder that none of us had ever met before the book club. Dumbfounded, I read the text message out loud.

"Dear Over-Fifty Book Club Members,

Thank you, dear M for initiating this stimulating and educational format for mature women to meet and discuss books! Carrie and I have thoroughly enjoyed meeting all of you. We have some exciting news: I am on the tarmac with Carrie. We are flying to Newfoundland to meet Carrie's parents! We are deeply in love. Our kids love each of their new 'mommies' as well. From Canada, we are moving to an innovative women's compound in San Miguel Allende in Mexico. What fun, eh?"

I continued breathlessly, "As you know, Carrie has been divorced from Tom for thirteen years and I never did find the right man. Turns out that's because I needed the Right Woman. And I have found her in my dear Carrie. It will be such a happy environment for our children.

So, we are off to the farm to raise goats and Brussels sprouts.

Happy reading! If you're ever in Mexico, please email us, we'd love to see you all (sans that scary lawyer lady, ha, ha,)

Thrills,

Mary Beth"

Our remaining four looked at me dumbfounded.

"No shit? Brussels sprouts? Ugh." That was Eleanor—choir mistress at her church, also known as Big Potty Mouth.

"Well...Carrie sounds like she's acting out," our resident psychiatrist offered.

"But she was *married*—with kids... is that well...normal?" Innocent Jill, from Iowa queried.

"Hey! Come on, we live in San Francisco. I just hope she realizes how hard it is to manage a goat. Not to mention both of their kids are about to be full-blown *teenagers*. I've tried to raise goats and *kids*... and it is hell."

Ever a worrywart, I, lamented, "Jeez, was it *my* book selection that drove them over the top? Remember how they both said it was a disturbing selection? I feel responsible."

Four pairs of eyes rolled at me, so I dropped the guilt trip. I guess that's what reading will do to you. That left the five of us who have been reading books, criticizing them, making theme dinners and drinking a lot of wine once a month for nearly ten years. I strongly suggest a book club. It's a great female version of a "beard" for drinking fests. just be sure to screen the applicants and maybe have a "probationary" period before you let someone into your kitchen–and every now and then read the book.

As part of our bonding experience, we decided to forgo a book one month and instead schedule a Spa day at a new modern high-end retreat. We joyfully went over the brochure. It sounded like Disneyland for tired "Mature" women. The name seems to wreak Calmness: *Forest Retreat Spa and Wellness Center*. I liked the *forest* and really wanted to be well. It offered a six-page menu of strange and delightful things that could be massaged, pounded, and poured over your body. Unfortunately, they offered healthy food lunches and snacks, but gratefully, they also had a full open bar that ran nine in the morning until ten thirty in the evening.

It was a different story when we arrived. I mean, the place was definitely serene. As in, Get-Me-Out-Of-This-Coma serene. Walls were painted what I can only describe as "uterine pink." I know about this because I learned in Psych 1 in college that many solitary confinement rooms are that same reassuring, Mommy-still-loves-you-no-matter-who-you-killed hue. It calms the savage beast and apparently, the Post-Menopausal Woman.

We were handed a detailed menu of the rubs and massages, and when I say "menu" I'm not kidding, because everything involved food–not *in* your body, but *on*. "Natural" yogurt was an intricate part of the program: one ate it, had facials with it, took baths in it, got scrubbed down with it and, well, drank it. Alcoholic beverages were offered with all forms of *yogurt*. There was a *Mint Green Yogurt Mojito. A Tequila Sunset Mango and Orange Mimosa,* and a sad little *Fresh Ground Spinach, Celery, Cilantro Bloody Mary*. It was an abusive way to mistreat alcohol.

I pulled myself away from the drinks and read out loud from the services brochure. I felt that it was our duty to ourselves to carefully examine each opportunity for Calmness and Wellness. I thought everyone would think that the yogurt treatments were pretty funny, but our choir leader and a former principal *and* currently an owner of restaurant thought it was just "sinful and wasteful and well, M., *stupid*."

She paused and then sighed, "Oh hell, think I'll try that yogurt mojito."

Our resident shrink, murmured, "I wonder what the meaning of all this food-as-treatment procedure *really* means…"

"I'm skipping the Probiotic culture–at least mixed with the booze, but maybe this 'Sturdy Little Vanilla Yogurt Scrub' would be good for me?" I raised an inquiring eyebrow. I wondered if maybe I should request a less-sturdy scrub…

The rest of the book gals demurred from the exotic treatments, opting for the Basic-Boring-Massages and uneventful mani-pedis. I however looked at the Papaya wrap, the Sugar Scrub, the Gentle Wash with Fruity Pectin Yogurt, the Walk into the River of Dreams and decided to go for broke. I bought the whole package—two-hundred dollars' worth of pampering. The scheduling lady, named I-swear-to-God, "Venus" warned me that the process would take three hours and I might miss their lunch offering. I thought about the flat, whole grain, hummus sandwiches photographed inside the menu, and shrugged, 'Oh, that's okay, I have this apple." I pulled out my Gala from Safeway. The woman shrank back in horror, "Is that ORGANIC? If not, I'm afraid I'll have to confiscate that from you."

"You've got to be kidding me, right?" *TSA?Here at the spa?*

Apparently, she was not, as she actually got up and came around the counter. I quickly popped the offensive, insecticide sprayed fruit back into my bag. I figured that I could always start licking my arms if I got hungry.

We got undressed in the communal dressing room or undressing room and slipped into our fluffy puffy bathrobes. I stuck my unauthorized apple into my pocket. We sat down on cushy chaise lounges and waited to be escorted for our services. An Agent-of-pleasure opened the door. She was shrouded in a pink sheet-like dress. Her hand firmly on my back, we piti-patted off to my various procedures.

The massage was first on the list. It was so relaxing that I nearly fell asleep. I think that there was some honey involved, but I really didn't mind. It was a good thing I didn't because I'd need to be on the alert for the rest of my "retreat into Heaven" package. Wrapped in my "Vanna Robe," I was led, weak-limbed, eyes fuzzy from oil—weather it was Olive or Canola I wasn't sure, dripping into my face, to The Grotto.

Obediently, I shuffled along in my spa slippers. I was passed over to a Grotto Goddess. No kidding, that was how they were referred. My escort had a name tag pinned to her that said she was "Goddess Amber." I think that was her name. I was too mesmerized by the draped thing that blossomed into bloomers around her skinny thighs. It kind of looked like a Greek version of a romper suit. She had long flaxen hair with a rather sci-fi looking flower protruding out of the side of head. Someone had paid a lot of money for orthodontics, because her teeth were perfect and white.

Flower-head girl exhaled breathlessly, "Hello, I'm Heather-Precious-Amber, your guide to the Grotto." She gently pushed me towards a sliding glass door. It was black-as-night inside, save for a weirdly throbbing amber light, barely visible in the floor. She gently grabbed my elbow and helped me mount stairs made of "stones" to a rock-covered table that to me, looked suspiciously like an altar. A teeny tiny scrap of a flattened-out pillow lay forlornly at the one end. She swiftly pulled on my robe tie. The robe slipped off into her waiting arms. I briefly worried about the Evil Apple in my pocket. The girl elbowed my butt until I got the message, and climbed upon the altar. I lay on my back, the little pancake pillow stuck to my hair. As I waited naked, slightly oiled up from the massage, I started to wonder if maybe a pedicure might have been a safer alternative.

Heather-Precious-Amber leaned above me and before I could say, "What-the-fuck?" *She* disrobed!

"Uh, hey, no. No, no, I don't want–"

"Shh," Grotto Goddess leaned across me, a very firm and pointy booby poking me in the eye. She extracted something from a jar and began vigorously rubbing me *everywhere*.

"No! Hey, what are you doing?"

From under my armpit she answered, "Scrubbing you. You will be beautifully exfoliated when I am finished."

"Yeah, OK....but you are *naked*."

"We find that we are more in sync with our clients if we are devoid of all artificial barriers."

"Well, my masseuse wasn't naked."

Heather-Precious-Amber gave a cute goat-like snort. "Oh but of course he was, you just didn't notice because you were so relaxed."

He? Naked? Gross. I felt violated. I remember the voice, melodic and smooth, instructing me to lay down. Had my masseuse been a man or a woman? And it *was* dark in there... *Well, hell, who cared if it was a man or woman? Naked was just not okay*. I tried to remember but I was getting too distraught because I was getting a weird burning tingling sensation.

Heather whispered against my shoulder, "So are you warm or cool?"

Was she talking about my color wheel? My personality? When I didn't respond, she extracted herself from my body, sat on the edge of the altar and informed me, "The Sugar scrub must be done while your body is at 99.9 degrees as well as the Papaya Scrub. We are wasting precious time. If we wait too long, I'll have to check your temperature and reheat the salve."

How do they discern the temperature? I didn't want her performing any "temperature checks" on me because I was very concerned about where the thermometer might go, so I blindly nodded my assent, mumbling, "I'm lovely…warm…thanks."

She attempted a frown "Are you sure?" I tried to pull back as she laid her palm on my forehead. I nodded numbly.

"Alrighty then." On the go signal, the girl went nuts. She jumped up on the altar and began to intensely rub my poor skin raw with the scrub. Once side one was done, she elbowed me onto my stomach and began pounding/scrubbing my ass with the sandpaper like concoction.

"Could we just skip this part?" I volunteered meekly.

"This is your Vigorous Scrub."

"Well, it hurts!" I whined.

No answer. Suddenly, she stopped. I heaved a sigh of relief then jolted as she sat up and announced, "And now, The Rain Part I!"

"Part I? What the hell–"

That's all that came out of my mouth because I had to shut it completely or drown as a deluge of water came pouring down from the ceiling. Squinting, I looked up and could barely distinguish what looked to be maybe thirty sprinklers. And they were not tiny rain-giving sprinklers. Oh no, these were *angry Gods* sprinklers that shot out fire-hose level gushes of water, stripping off my eye makeup in less than thirty seconds and removing the first layer of my skin at the same time. Grotto Goddess was standing near the sliding door exit, (a place I was determined to get to somehow). She too, had been pelted by gigantic globs of the alleged raindrops, but she was smiling like an idiot.

"OK, that's enough of tha'" I gurgled, rubbing sugar out of my eyes and a clump of hair from my cheek.

She ignored me and grabbing a bucket, leaped up on the altar-of-discomfort and using a paintbrush, started slathering something sticky and tingling on to my quivering legs.

"This is the Papaya. In a minute, you will be wrapped and the infusing heat will penetrate."

Penetrate? I'm a married woman. I really didn't like her language. I wasn't interested in being steamed, wrapped, infused or penetrated unless my husband was involved. Before I could protest, the sliding door opened. I sat up, with hope. Wafts of fresh chilling air came in along with a new Goddess. She was in a two-piece ensemble that consisted of a loincloth and bra top. She handed the crazy naked girl a robe and then turned to me and exclaimed,

"Now you will be wrapped and all of the nutrients of the Universe will be absorbed."

"No thank you," I squeaked.

Didn't work. She shook out what looked like a roll of paper towels. They were not paper towels.

"Wha's tha'?" I was having some serious trouble articulating my words. There really was this weird tingling at the back of my throat. I lifted a hand in panic, pointed to my throat and gurgled, "I think tha' I'm allergic to papaya."

Goddess in bloomers ignored me and with a flick of her well-cut arm, unrolled a mighty length of what turned out to be hand woven gauze from some godforsaken island off of North Africa. Faster than a gift wrapper at Macys, she rolled me up in the organic-would-be-cheese cloth. Within three minutes I looked like a mummy. I smelled like a Thai salad. I lay immobilized on the altar. Frankly, I was scared shitless. I kept thinking of my friends with their happy pink toes and pushed back cuticles.I lifted my stiff neck up to beg for release.

New Goddess stepped back and fluttered her eyes, "Now, enjoy the STEAM." The way she enunciated I thought that maybe the original God of Steam was coming in. Then she vanished. I heaved a sigh of relief that my torturer was gone. It was pitch black except for that throbbing light on the floor. I kept my eyes focused where I had last seen the sliding door. As laid on my bed-of-pain, I whimpered like a wimp.

Then, there was a sudden violent hissing sound.

"Holy crap! Is there a fuckn' snake in here?! Help! Hel-lo? Help!!" I tried to stand up, but not in time. Not that there would be any standing—remember I was wrapped up like a papaya-with-tuna and sand sushi roll.

Suddenly, the hiss became a roar and steam started to come down from the ceiling.

"Oh, not the damn ceiling thing again! No!"

As if steam, that was as thick as a volcano's vent wasn't enough, it started oozing out of the floor as well. I felt like I was about to be serviced with capital punishment. I blinked my eyes, searching for an exit. Wasn't that California law? There had to be an exit sign somewhere. The steam was accompanied by an ominous pounding sound. As if a full-blown dragon was going to join me in my little mini rock cave. Great gray clouds of mist that smelling sickly like vanilla pudding gone bad belched out of the floor and above me.

Within minutes I could hardly breath and I went into a full-blown panic attack. Writhing like a silk worm in a cocoon, I wriggled myself off the rock bed, banged my head on the artificial stone, and rolled over to the sliding door. Now I was Uma Thurman in Kill Bill Two, trapped in the coffin. *Where the hell were my knife and my matches?*

"Help!" my voice sounded like a cartoon character's squeaky pathetic plea. I craned my neck to look down at my toes that were swelling into Barney Rubble stumps. In a few minutes, I assumed that all of my circulation would be cut off and I would die there, a pot-sticker amongst the insane.

The mist evaporated for a second and I spied the sliding glass door. I rolled-writhed toward it just in time to be assaulted by another vent of angry steam.

Depleted, I laid listlessly by the slider. There was the tinniest fraction of the door opened. Using my nose, I managed to inch the door open.

Wanly, I pleaded, "Hello, please save me."

No answer. I promised myself to never eat crab again, fully understanding what it felt like to be steamed alive.

After what seemed like an eternity, the original Goddess appeared on the other side of the sliding door.

"Oh, now look *at you!*" Vaguely annoyed that she had found me squirming at her feet, her tone made me feel like I was a puppy, or in this case, a crustacean, who'd made a poo-poo on the floor.

She exhaled dramatically, and hoisted me by my armpits and practically flung me on to the first step of the rocks. She was a surprisingly strong little thing. While I was limply propped up against the top step, she unwrapped me. Naked, humbled, beaten down by violent water and choking steam, I shuffled behind her as she led me to a door I had not seen. An invisible door! No shit. The damn thing was painted the same color as the rock wall. To think that there had been an *escape route.* Of course, by that time, I'd lost the will-to-live and was well, papaya jelly in her evil hands.

"Come with me."

She ordered, I obeyed. I was clearly into post-traumatic syndrome.

I crossed the threshold into another rocky structure, this time a hallway, aka, a Long Rock Tunnel. The door behind me slammed shut and Goddess was on the other side. At last, I was safe.

I was wrong. So, wrong.

Through a creepy speaker imbedded into a fake rock, I heard her gleefully announce, "And now we have RAIN, Part II."

"Oh, for Christ's sakes, give me a break!" I protested, but not soon enough. I turned around, reached out, searching for a hidden doorknob. I was alone in a long dark cave. How the hell had they built this scare ride in the middle of San Francisco? Did they actually issue building permits for torture?

The rock-tunnel-rain-trap was black as night–again. Then I heard a low murmur, then a gurgle and then a grumbling sound. Genuine terror rose up in me. An H2O assault began. Rain? No, deluge! At the same time, bright lights came on. I started running down the pretend cave, waving my hands in the air like a crazy woman, cursing the gigantic killer rain-drops. At the end of the tunnel, the "rain" stopped. Soft lights blinked on, revealing towels and a new bathrobe on hooks waiting. I mourned the loss of my apple; a weak attempt at rebellion. There was annoying chiming musical notes being piped in from some rock. The towels were fluffy, warm and way too small for a normal sized woman. I was so sticky and grainy that I had to take a shower before I could leave the area.

Overwhelmed, I stumbled to the dressing room. My fingers were pump and wrinkled like an old lady's. My ears had sugar and something orange in them. I seriously wasn't sure I could stand to take another shower, but I still had salad fixings all over my body and in my hair. I had to wash it four times before it looked like hair again. I also managed to wash all my hair dye out. When I emerge from my experience, I found the girl friends lounging on chaises, wiggling their happy red and French man-icured toes. Everyone was partaking of a lovely green pitcher of Margaritas. Wisely, the carafe of water with dead pieces of cucumber and I think, broccoli, was ignored.

My friends' eyebrows went up.

"Wow, you look really. . . PINK."

"And, err…M., why did you have them remove your color? "

"Huh?" I think I gurgled that one out, as I coughed up a wad of papaya.

One of the ladies gestured towards the floor-to-ceiling mirror. "M., I don't think I like you au natural, girl!"

I studied the gray-haired, water-peeled reflection in front of me. That damn treatment had not only removed my makeup and part of my skin, but my hair color as well. I looked like I was, well, fifty-eight.

"You look very relaxed though," one offered diplomatically. She reached over and poured a glass of water with the limp cucumber floating in it. "But maybe all that rubbing dehydrated you–they say you should drink extra water."

I glared back at the offending glass, and cringed when she attempted to hand it to me. "No!" I got a hold of myself as they all looked at me in alarm, "No thank you, *no water.*"

Apparently, no one understood that I'd just been pummeled nearly to death by the water death squad. Oblivious to my pain and shock, they all stood up and a barrage of questions began.

"So, how was the massage?"

"And the wrap?"

I rolled a stray papaya seed out of my mouth, poured myself a very large margarita and spat, "Don't ask."

"But wasn't it fabulous? "

I have my pride you know, so I forced a smile and sighed, "Invigorating."

So, I guess I'm not the exotic spa type personality. I agree with my friend. Food should go *in* your body, not on.

It took a couple of meetings and the psychiatrist in our group observing that I cringed every time I was offered a glass of water, for me to finally share my PTSD incident with the book club. We vowed to venture away from our local salons and to pursue only our love of gossiping, griping, reading and of course, drinking wine. And of course, our love—of books and each other. Again, it's always about Love.

CHAPTER ELEVEN

Two Feet, but So Many Possibilities...

I LOVE MY FAMILY, I LOVE MY FRIENDS. I LOVE TO WRITE and read, but *shopping* I really enjoy. It really became fun when I could at last spend money at *Nordstrom's*, not at Ikea. Not that any kind of shopping isn't fun and even Ikea was charming. You have to have a college-bound child to understand the wonder of Ikea. That store is the haven for dorm-furnishings. This clever Swedish company has figured out the formula: a vast, rather frightening-overwhelming box, filled with every color imaginable of modern, well-priced furniture and kitschy fun accessories. If your child likes pink polka dot shower curtains, Ikea has them and matching towels, area rug and towel cabinet.

What you discover as you're pushing your gigantic shopping cart through endless aisles of endless possibilities, is that anything larger than what you could throw into that cart, must be picked out and *up* by yourself and worse, assembled on site of said domicile. Having two daughters in college dorms, and then their "own" apartments, which of course we paid for way past college graduation day, I did my fair share of dolling out the dollars, schlepping huge pieces of laminated book cases up flights of stairs, and ultimately having to purchase my very own tool kit.

It was a rare time when I could be a selfish brat and just buy something frivolous for me–just because I am *me*. Hence, I entered my late-shopping phase with a vengeance. For a while, it became a fun past time. I'd scour fashion magazines. My youngest would have been so proud. I also stared at "cool looking" moms at coffee shops. I watched. I learned. However, nothing really inspired me. Since my experience with The Purse, I was cautious. And I admit, I was still sadly attached to my "vintage" jeans.

There was one thing I really wanted to get. For a long time, especially after working in the Very Expensive Shoe Store, I had wanted some *Manalos*. When Niemen Marcus had a sale, I joined a friend and we pretty much went crazy. I bought three pairs. Mind you, I could hardly put them on my poor-retail-killed-my-feet, but I didn't care. I let the salesman, my shopping buddy, and myself convince me that they'd "loosen up" or I could just get my toes removed.

When I got home, I lined them up on top of our bed and I, well, I just *stared* at them. Perfection in leather. They were like little size nine art pieces. Never mind that they were actually NOT little. . .

After a few days of admiration, I tried them on again. I squashed my bunion-callus-corn-feet into them and stared down in dismay. They were terribly painful. They had not hurt THAT much at the store or had I been drunk on sale-euphoria? I looked at the bottom of the sales slip, below the ghastly total, where it stated in bold letters that there were *no return possibilities.* I knew I could challenge that, but I also knew better than to humiliate myself by attempting to return them. After all, I'd been on the giving end of distain while working at the Very Expensive Shoe Store, so I knew better. In addition, I admit it, I *loved* those shoes—every single pair that barely fit. I wanted them, pain or no pain. I could limp from the damn car to the restaurant, right?

I recalled one of the salespeople from work telling me about the legendary shoe repair icon, Amazari Shardarsi. Amazari's Shoe Repair was the best. In the world of disposable, cheap crap, he existed to serve the few who purchased expensive things and wanted them repaired. He was a rare species. His was a lost art. He mended shoes, bags and belts. *He could also stretch shoe sizes up two notches.* He could make my feet glamorous.

I drove up to his store and then spent twenty minutes driving around the block, trying to find parking. There was a line into his shop that extended past two other store fronts. I wondered if he was giving away shoes? I trotted up (in my tennis shoes of course) to que up behind a matron standing beside a younger lady. I gawked at the girl, dressed in a grey maid's uniform, as she struggled to balance her hold on two Barney's bags, a Niemen's bag and two Saks' bags, all of them piled to the top with high-end shoe boxes. *Maid? People actually make their servants dress like this, jeez...* I duly noted that none of the boxes looked to be from the Very Expensive Shoe Store.

I made an anemic attempt to chit chat the matrons. They looked me over from my pill-covered sweater down to my tennis shoes. They'd have none of me. I managed to strike up a stilted conversation with one of the carriers. Her response to my bantering was to nod, shrug and grimace. Apparently, she was too afraid to lose focus on the objective of staying in line. After about thirty minutes, one of the Rich Owners of Shoes, abandoned her employee and announced that she was going shopping (hopefully not for more shoes,) and she'd be back.

"I certainly hope that you are in the shop by then!" she extolled, as if the poor woman left holding her greed-bags was the one causing the hold up.

The line slowly inched forward. Once inside, a blowzy gal with long hair and a kind of belly-dancing costume laid over sweater and trousers, handed me a maple piece of wood with a number on it. The wood was shaped like a high-heeled shoe. I chuckled, *pretty cute.* I stopped laughing when I noted that my number was *thirty-five.* I looked around at the crowded store, stuffed with sighing, impatient customers. I joined their sighs with my own exhale and leaned against a case of old abandoned shoes with a warning note on the top: *These could be yours!*

Don't be late picking up your shoes! We leave them here for you to see, but NEVER have back!

I imagined returning for a forgotten pair of shoes, being told they were in that case, and too bad, you can't have them. *Weird. Was that even legal?*

Another fifteen minutes and I finally made it to the counter. Amazari was swarthy, dressed in what looked like a silk smoking jacket, with an industrial leather apron tied around his waist. He had a beard that tickled the top of his apron. He reeked of some kind of sweet smoke. He had huge bushy black eyebrows overhanging piercing gold eyes. He looked like a scary version of a genie.

I set the bag of my shoes on the counter.

"What is it that you want, eh?"

I personally thought that was kind of stupid. I mean wasn't it obvious that I needed my shoes repaired? I extracted my boxes and laid the neatly in a row.

Amazari whipped the lids off and tossed them on the floor and peered into the boxes.

Whoa, I paid good money for those boxes and lids. I took a breath, "Well, I need these stretched. They are too tight"

"Why you buy them if they don't fit?" White teeth gleamed under the beard–and I noted his sneering tone. He squinted his beady eyes at me knowingly.

Before I could answer he gave a low grumble and muttered, "Of course, on *sale* yes?"

I felt like I was in a Shopaholic Anonymous meeting. I hung my head in shame and mumbled, "Uh huh. But they're Manalo's"

He pulled the shoes out, "Mano-shmmo–who cares? It they hurt, they aren't worth shit, right?" He grabbed some kind of stapler thing, tagged each shoe with a color strip and tossed my precious babies over his shoulder.

I jerked up and reached my arm out to intercept him. "My shoes! Did that thing puncture my shoes? You can't throw Manalos around!"

He snorted and then chuckled, "Relax lady, it makes a *tiny* hole, very precise. "

All I heard was the word *hole*. "The boxes are—-"

He interrupted me with a snort, "I have *hundreds* of these boxes. I'll put them right back into a Niemen Marcus box when I'm done, or maybe you'd like a Bonwit Taylor instead, eh?" Mean laugh again.

"No, my own box. Wait," I inched around the corner and gathered the symbols of my sales-triumph, "I'll just take the boxes home, if you don't mind." *If he was so damn good with putting things back into boxes why did he have so many boxes lying around?*

He shrugged and replied, "Well, you don't mind putting nice shoes in plastic bag, I don't give a shit either."

"But they have their own special bag, see?" I fished out a soft flannel bag from the discarded box.

"I keep track of the *shoes*, Miss, not the bags or boxes for that matter." He shrugged and gave me an intense stare. Meanwhile, I could hear female rumblings behind me.

I was exhausted and wanted to just get out of there. Finally, I checked in what would have retailed not on sale for approximately twenty-five hundred dollars' worth of shoes. Before he handed me my receipt, he told me that I had to pay up front. *One hundred and sixty-five dollars.*

When I started to protest, the man snarled, "You get *these* for free? No? Then I don't work for free. Maybe you never come back, and I'm stuck with shitty shoes that are size nines!" His eyes slid to the case of abandoned shoes and he jerk his chin at me.

I looked around me shamed-face that I had such big feet for such a short woman. Now it had been publically broadcasted. Worse yet, they were now being stretched into larger clown feet. "When can I have them back?" I was contrite like a little kid.

Amazari promised me them back, and stretched, in "around one or two weeks, I'm a busy guy. I work alone."

"When *exactly* should I come by?" I pressed on, and looked anxiously behind him at the pile upon pile of Pradas, Michael Kors and Jimmy Choos. They were all jumbled on top of each other, with little tags projecting out of their insides like so many cows at the slaughter-house. It didn't seem the right way to treat such expensive shoes, but he *was* the best, right? Anyway, I just wanted a commitment on when my *shitty shoes* would be done.

Amazari, threw his muscular arms up in the air, shoved a little orange tag with numerals on it into my clenched fist, and waved me towards the door and the street, all the while he chanted, "I call you, I call you. Don't call me!"

"OK, OK." *The man's an artist.*

I exercised self-control and did not call him.

Nor did he call me.

Two weeks went by and no call. I retrieved the claim tag out of my wallet and starred at it. *I call you, I call you.* I posted it on the frig.

Three weeks, and I broke the rule and called him. No answer. No voice mail.

I shared my concern with my friend Emma.

"Oh, no worries honey; he probably went to the Old Country to visit his family." We all called his country of origin the "old country" because he was of unidentifiable ethnic descent. Some people thought he was Syrian. Others, Persian, had not answered his phone.

I waited another week and I dialed his number. Panic set in when I got the "this number has been disconnected" message.

I decided to drive out to his shop.

The shop was no more. What was left was a pile of burned timber, a sign and tipped over cash register and a guy in a white jumpsuit sweeping debris.

"Oh-my-god! What happened to Amazari?"

"Oh, he's in jail."

"What?" I felt my stomach knotting up

"Well, there are some questions about the fire."

"Fire?" I gripped his arm.

The man frowned at me and shook me off, then made a broad gesture, "Hel-lo? Fire? Don't you notice the extreme lack of a building behind me, duh."

I was speechless and just stared at him, dumbfounded. Of course, from his perspective, I guess I just looked plain stupid. I walked slowly over to the caution tape wall that surrounded what used to be where I last saw my shoes. It was a crime scene alright. I stepped under the tape, and stretched my neck, vainly searching for my shoes' bodies.

"Hey—no! Lady, you can't go there. Stay on this side of the barrier, please." He jumped up behind me.

"But my shoes…" I looked up at him and he shook his head

"Nothing here now but ashes and soot. Don't you watch the local news? His store burned down about two weeks ago. He was having some problems making his lease and getting customers and–"

"He had a line wrapped around the block with customers. I don't understand; *I* was a customer, and a good one. He has all of my new shoes!"

"Really?" He leaned on the broom and smirked, "I think the operative word would be *had,* not has. Got a receipt?" Creepy Clean Up Guy jutted his chin towards the rubble and chuckled, "not that it'll do much good. You can contact the police. I dunno if they can help or not."

Oh shit.

I became part of a mini-class action suit of pathetic broads who tried to collect from Mr. Shardarsi. Only problem was that he had nothing to collect. He never went to jail either. Left the United States for the *Old Country.* I still don't have a clue where that might have been. I personally think that was New Jersey.

Fortunately, I had some weird rider on my homeowners that covered "loss by incompetence" and I got reimbursed. I presumed they were referring to *my* incompetence. Well, I got a check for the total I spent. Of course, that money doesn't even come close to what the shoes were worth, not just the money, but the too-priceless-to-describe-ego soothing aspects, as well. I guess now I'll just have to wait ions for another bargain sale like that one. This was just not my day to enjoy the love, in this case, my love of shoes.

CHAPTER TWELVE

Jealousy—the Elixir of Life or Forget Half, I'll take Jail

HITTING YOUR SIXTIES IS VERY TRAUMATIC. YOU REALLY can't get your panties-lined-with-a-panty-liner-in-case-you-sneeze, in a twist when the box boy calls you "Mam." The jig is up. You are most definitely a "mam." Virtually *everyone* who waits on you could be your potential illegitimate child. I pretty much hate anyone under the age of forty. Once I confessed to this in the mirror, I embraced it. I'm not bitter. I am *envious*. Why does smooth skin have to be wasted on someone who never checks their pores, only their smart phone?

Speaking of phones, I almost dread getting phone calls from my friends; husband's got prostate cancer, reading glasses aren't working, bulging stomach, breast lumps or just sagging boobs, feet hurting, weird things on your face. The cures are just as terrifying; MOHS surgery (mostly on noses –a sick funny joke), radiation, proton therapy, and angiograms. You name it. The diagnosis and the cures have a way of scaring the crap out of you. One friend of mine has solved the problem: she hasn't been to a doctor in five years. Clearly, she's just scared shitless to find out what she might be dying of.

Everyone jokes about it the joys of aging. At fifty if you're still having sex it is great. At sixty, if you can laugh without peeing in your pants, you're happy. At seventy, if you have sense of humor left, you're pleased and at eighty, if any of your friends are still around, it's a good day. We all just hang in there and spend a lot of time laughing at ourselves, or spouses, of course.

I can tell you that I miss the *Other Version of my Hubby* at his hey-day, when he was finally bringing in the big bucks, got the car, the house, went to the health club before he came home. Back in the good old days, after we got rid of the kids, we'd share wine and have pretty decent sex. Menopause had its value. We finally no longer worried about birth control. However, by the time the poor thing was in his sixties, the only six figures he's collecting is the ID number on his social security check, (yes, there's *nine* numbers, but he can only recall six…) and his wobbly pension fund. My friend tells me that her husband can't see his "business" down there because he's too blind and it's partially blocked by his stomach. He pretty much leaves her alone if she hides the Viagra pills in the laundry basket.

We women however fight back with a vengeance. If there's any money to be had, we usually have had a facelift, or an eye-lift, or a tummy tuck or at least, five gallons of Botox and filler by then, so we've pretty much halted time at say "fiftyish."

So maybe that explains why all of a sudden, it's the *gals* running away. I had three friends "suddenly" dump their husbands and run off, with half of not much, and wind up in the same apartment they were living in forty years ago. One friend called me to say that she could hardly wait to hit the dating sites and "get laid." *Really?* I think that they fool themselves into thinking that just because *their* saggy jowls have been delegated to the top of their heads, their lips jammed full of silicone, that they actually *are* younger. You can't disguise your whole body and for sure, the internal parts inevitably turn on you.

I for one don't get it. I mean really, who the hell wants to start dating at sixty-something? Now, I always used to tell my husband, "Honey, if I have cancer and I'm dying in three months that gives *you* one month to live because I will kill you. You see, no other woman is going to be living in my house or wearing my jewelry."

I've seen it, so I'm a bit sensitive on this issue. Friend of mine died of breast cancer. Poor Bill. He was a wreck. He couldn't do the bills or make a meal because my dear friend Evie had done it all. I mean it. Right up to the day before she died, she was balancing the check book and filling out the insurance forms. She even made up six frozen casseroles. Yes, *really*. She was worried he'd starve to death after she died. And what happened to the grieving widower? Married. Within six months that fool is going to Vegas with the twenty-something checker he met at Wal-Mart who told him that she just loved men who wear generic underwear. *Uh huh.*

However, in that case, karma was a bitch. Saw Bill at the grocery store and asked him how is new wife was. He shrugged his shoulders and answered sheepishly, "Err…we got an annulment."

Ha! I couldn't help myself. "What happen, Bill?"

Silence accompanied by his shuffling his feet and then, I felt Evie cheering from above."Well, she wasn't a *she*. She was a *he*, or a shim, I guess. Anyway…"

I suppressed my guffaw and shook my head, "So you couldn't work it out?" I bit my lip, wondering if that was kind of a sick pun?

Bill raised his brows and shook his head, "Nah, we really didn't have that much in common anyway."

Ha! Again.

"Guess I should have waited before…oh well. See you." Poor Bill slithered away.

I die first and my man get remarried before the grass has grown over my plot? No siree! Not on my watch. All these ladies who say, "Oh if I died, I want him to get remarried…" Blah, blah, blah. *Negatory.*

Yes, I can be a mean bitter bitch, but let's get real. If a man just *has* to have a replacement wife, because he's a total incompetent in the house then he should at least wait a year. I mean three hundred and sixty-five days of old casseroles and take out is not too much to ask as an atonement for all those times he rejected your overcooked roast. Let me add that daughters, clear out the jewelry before the old man starts dating again. I did despicable things in bed with your father for those one-carat earrings.

Now we know that the poor males most likely die before their spouses, so you might ask, what about us? I always say to my hubby, "Oh honey, if you died, I'd never remarry. Why would I want a Chevy when I've had a Mercedes?"

He loves it when I talk like that. It's better than talking dirty, believe me. And besides, they don't need to know about your plan to buy a Porsche and drive to Las Vegas without sunscreen, believe me. Seriously, most widows don't remarry—must be a reason—*you* figure that one out.

Don't get me wrong, I adore my hubby. Mine is wonderful and very useful. He carries packages. I can call on him any time of the day to murder a spider. Some husbands fix things. *Mine* does not do that too well. He's better at writing checks. We have a screen door at the back of the house that is still hanging upside down and my daughter's closet has the remnants of a closet unit jammed sideways into the wall.

However, he has single-handedly chopped off the head of a rattlesnake with a garden hoe (believe me, he relives that one continuously.) Frankly, the memory of him holding that dead snake, dripping in disgusting snake blood, is still a real turn-on. My husband also gives great presents. He is the master of surprise and it's endearing. In addition, he has braved 30-degree weather to cheer his girls on the soccer field, and picked icicles out of his daughter's hair during swim meets in Colorado, Kansas and the lovely Wyoming.

The man is generous to a fault. When Thing One was thirteen, we sent her to Space Camp. She had a two-hour layover in Chicago and managed to discharge all of her spending money at the airport. I yelled at her, husband gently reminded her that she needed to be more prudent. Then he promptly refilled her bankcard. I am happy in my role as the Bitch Mean Mother, foiled by The Good and Kind Papa.

The money issues have gone on for years. The girls spend, the Papa refills. It's so blatant that Thing One made him a T-shirt for Father's Day that had an ATM machine on the front and the back said, "FUNDS." Funny, but not so funny. We are waiting to get even. At this rate, we'll spend everything we've got and show up at our children's door. That is to say, we hope they have a door—other than the car door.

Let's talk about jealousy, insecurity, and necessity. Yes, I admit it, I've had my share of jealous fits and I feel no shame, except that I didn't follow through with a punch in a jaw in lieu of an actual murder. I will never forget one of my husbands' mistakes, or as *he* refers to it, "lack of judgement." First mistake he made was hiring an attractive cheap-looking secretary. Caught her ass-grabbing my husband in public, right in front of me. Now this is sacred territory. Ass grabbing involves at least *silver* jewelry in our house, so needless to say, I was very concerned.

We were at a company party. I was doing my wifely duty and mixing it up, when I look across the room, I see my husband flushing, his martini trembling in his hands and his buttock firmly in the hands of his new assistant. According to Husband, he swears that he looked around embarrassed and mumbled, "M., take your hands off my behind, there is no diamond ring in there," and that's when he looked around the room to see who was catching us and saw *me* across the way glaring at him. Imagine his shock (and flattered ego) when he whirled around to see *who* was indeed fondling his butt.

Clearly this woman had no idea who I was or *could be*. That same evening, I finally lost it when I watched her teeter towards my man and comment on his absence that day (he'd had dental extraction done that morning.)

Her way of expressing concern was to lean over, press her boobs into his throat and stick her finger into his own numbed-out mouth and exclaim, "Oh, you poor thing, is it all red and sore?"

I froze there, standing right beside him, wondering first, how she could be so stupid and then, did we have the death penalty in California? *That's it! Something is going to be red and sore!*

I don't know what made me more furious: her fingers inside his mouth or his dumb-chicken lack of protest. He claims that he was just too shocked by her weird behavior. He added that he was brain-numb from the post-anesthesia and the martini. I accepted that and moved in to rescue him. In a very lady like manner, as any corporate wife should behave, I politely came over, whispered into her bleach-fried hair that unless she wanted some dental surgery of her *own*, she should extract her fake boobs from his neck and her fingers from his mouth.

She drew back shocked, but did not even have the sense to be chagrined at all. She just murmured, with a sigh like Marilyn Monroe in heat, "Oh, I didn't know he was married and to *you*."

AS IF I HAD A LIFE

"Yep. He is. And so is his ass that you were fondling earlier. Say, do you type?"

"Of course." She pouted at me and batted her fake lashes.

"Great. I suggest that you go home tonight or into the car you live in, and type a really nice resignation letter. That way I won't have to come into *my* husband's office tomorrow and cause a big ruckus by kicking your skinny ass out." "I don't think it's legal to talk to me that way." She narrowed her Other Woman baby blues, and jutted her too-cute-but-breakable chin at me.

"Wanna find out? I guess you haven't heard about me. *I. AM. CRAZY*. Besides, you tramp, I don't work here." I turned to look at my husband with triumph, but he had wisely fled the scene. Probably for the best.

Now, I had mastered this "crazy thing" way back. When you're in your forties, usually we girls have to worry about the man leaving us for some hot eighteen-year-old who's noticed that he's making six figures while *your* chasing *his* kids around, feeling like and looking like, you're the walking dead. So, any threats must be met with aggressive nutty action.

It worked. She never showed up for work again. Floozy secretary flew out of town—to Vegas. My husband's next assistant was a gay man whom I adored as we could go shopping together during his lunch break.

I got to admit, that getting all those passive-aggressive feelings out was cathartic, really. The added bonus was that my kids were really proud of me. My friends were astounded and inspired. I was the new heroine of the neighborhood. Now once my husband got over his fear of me, he admitted that he was actually rather flattered that I cared so much.

"I was amazed at your...er...*passion*. I never knew you could be so possessive" He gave me a careful hug.

I gave him a smug smile and a patted him on the shoulder. "Just another form of love, that's all. But no more floozy assistants, right honey?"

From then on, just as a preventative measure, I'd come down to "visit" every now with my friend's younger kids, pretending that they were *my* under-age-need-vast-child-support-payments-children, and draped in most of my entire jewelry box. Message: if you want him, just try, but I'm getting more than *half—that is if I let him live."*

As you hit your sixties, the stories of your kids have morphed into tales of weird behaviors from people's semi-adult kids. Once they got past eighteen, it was supposed to be less aggravating, not more. As they moved to adulthood, it becomes an additional lesson in continual humility. I wanted to live my children's lives. No, not to help them avoid mistakes, because *I want their damn lives!* I want arms that are not bat wings, and a tush that doesn't look like Sponge Bob's body. I'd get the agitated phone calls from my lady friends: Little Used-to-be Perfect Johnny who was enrolled in Stanford Medical school had gone and lost his mind. He had ran off with some Thai chick who was supposed to be a radiologist and they both had fled to Bangkok and were *studying* massage therapy. My friend Abby's charming daughter quit her job at a major internet firm, deposited her two boys with Abby, and announced she was in love with her gynecologist, and ran off with *her*.

My adult children, so far have thankfully remained relatively boring. I still go shopping with my youngest, now an adult-type person, but with a very a cold heart. I was planning a trip to a spa with her dad, so I was checking out yoga get-ups. I knew enough not to have a totally pink yoga suit, but I tried on the happy pink pants, with a tasteful grey zip-up top with pink piping.

I pranced around the fitting room.

I did a down-dog. "What do you think? Aren't these cute?"

Droll voice: "Umm. . . Mom, don't lean over like that." I scowled at her. "I'm doing yoga."

"Right."

I ignored her and asked, "What about these darling pants?" I wiggled my semi-toned ass in the air.

She cringed and enunciated: "They are P.I.N.K."

"But they're so cute."

"If you're six years old, Moth-er." Seeing my fallen face, she asked kindly, "Do you *want* to look ridiculous?"

Alrighty then, black yoga pants it is.

I suppose that from *her* perspective, it was about the love...

CHAPTER THIRTEEN

You Can Lead a Horse to Water, and You Can Beat It to Death—Quasi-Adult Children and Other Myths

THING TWO WAS IN HER SECOND YEAR OF COLLEGE. SHE IS a very smart girl. She was also a rather dramatic young adult. She actually doubled majored in the private-college-we-ended-up-paying-*full-price*-for-because-the-full-ride-college-in-the-deep-South-was-just-too-*hot*. Totally understandable; one doesn't want to melt while waiting for one's iced lattes, non? And ice lattes she had indeed. In fact, her little "food card" that we judiciously loaded up on automatic deposit was creatively used for lots of things besides food. Local vendors had made a deal with the school, so that nail salons, hairdressers, gourmet coffee shops and bakeries off campus were all part of the "student experience, and *relating to the community.*" A sweet deal for all—err, for *someone.* Hence, she played and dined well in Los Angeles, while we, her parents, refrained from lattes, good wine and movies in order to make the tuition deduction. By the way, this money is taken out of your checking account faster than a gold-digger on her way to a widowers' convention. But hey, it's the love, right?

Well, it would be okay except, that apparently, as your child goes through his/her separation and independence development, an odd thing happens. Thing Two became very independent. At least she *sounded* independent. Well, let's say *cheeky.* Okay, make that *obnoxious.* For example, I phoned her, because she had been "dark" for three weeks. Texting wasn't a "thing" yet, so verbal communication was still around. However, not for me: no phone calls. Nada.

So, being the neurotic mother I am, I phoned *her.* The conversation went something like this:

"Hi Honey, it's me, Mommy."

"*Duh.* What do you want Mom?"

Err…. love? "Just checking on you. Haven't heard from you." *In almost a month, you twit!*

"Be-cause. I. AM. VERY. BUSY." This was followed by a very protracted sigh and I just know that there was a double hair-toss, eye-rolling in there as well.

"So, did you get the care-box I sent?" I tried not to sound too hopeful.

Let me explain this care-box thing. At the orientation for freshmen parents, it was *strongly* suggested that parents send a box of *special* things from home that symbolized our love and support, because of this myth that the freshmen actually *miss* their families. I can tell you now, that no way do they miss their families. They might miss a home-cooked meal and their laundress, but not *you*.

In the box were items suggested by the school counselors that should include "comfort food" and special little gifts. I packed homemade cookies, which I haven't done in four years, but I did, lovingly sealed up in zip lock bags and placed in a cute container covered with pictures of her family-that-she-did-not-miss. Also included were a cute pair of sunglasses. I figured I'd get points on that gesture as she was in southern California, squinting up at fabulous sunlight. I also included a bikini (like how cool am I, right?), sunscreen (all right, not *that* cool,) and pictures of the dogs, the cats, her older sister, her Papa, and a tiny candid one of her and I at an amusement park. All this was packaged and sent via Fed-Ex (as we were told that US Cheap Mail, is often "unreliable") for a total of fifty-five dollars, and what response did I get?

"Yes." Oh yeah, and "duh."

Hmm.... so far, so good. When you are a parent of a quasi-adult, *whole* words are highly valued. You don't even expect an entire sentence. It's as if the child was a toddler again and first talking.

Encouraged, I plowed on. "And?"

"And, *hel-lo*? I ate the cookies."

"What about the bathing suit? The sunscreen? The glasses? The pictures?" I was so close to whining that I had to take a breath. I felt like the ugly girl in the lunchroom. *No one wants to talk to me. Do I exist?* But I didn't let go. "Did the suit fit?"

"Yes."

Now my voice had dropped to a whisper. "Do you like it?"

"Sure Mom, but don't buy me anymore clothes okay? I'll just use my allowance."

Oh yeah, your generous over-the-top-allowance. "You didn't like the color" My voice is absolutely whiny and accusatory. "Moth-er. It. Is. *Pink*. What's up with you and *pink*? I've *told* you, Mommy: pink is for six year olds."

"Oh, sorry." *Shit, I was a loser again.*

"But the sunglasses are awesome. Are those really Chanel? "

And like the great mother I wanted to be, I lied. "Absolutely. *Only the best for you sweetie*." I figured that since she acted like a bitch, I must have some of that in me, as well, right? *Payback. Truth is not always best.*

"Err... thank you. Are you okay Mom? You sound weird."

Now I was the weird one. Fine, so I ended the conversation.

A couple of days later, I got a random bill for some miscellaneous expense not deducted from our checking account. It's something about the recreation center and cafeteria—I don't know, I had kind of lost the will to live at that point, and I just paid it. Sometimes I felt as if I were writing an alimony check to my husbands' non-existent ex-wife. I supposed that this must be what it's like to have a semi-hostile female in your family that you got to send cash too, eh?

Two months later, I get a letter from the school. I should be so proud, so happy, and so broke. Below is the letter (the italics are my attempt at irony.)

> Your daughter, Thing Two, has been selected for the opportunity to travel to China for a year to study. With the *reasonable* additional cost of $4000, she will be allowed to immerse herself in the community of China. During this unique experience, she will reside at the University of Beijing, housed with students from all over the world, and of course, Chinese nationals.

> Please be advised that your regular tuition payments will continue to be deducted from your checking account, as this is an *enrichment* program.

> The group will depart April 1 at SFO, United Airlines terminal, promptly at 1:45 P.M.

> *(Let me add here, that since April 1 was the onset of Spring break, parents whose children might actually live in Los Angeles or not even planning to leave campus, still had to get their children to San Francisco for this excursion.)*

> All students must be at the airport and the below designated meet-up area at 11:00 A.M.

Students must submit a cleared passport, and visa to be obtained prior to the trip and presented to the travel coordinator no later than March 1.

All students must bring the attached list of clothing and toiletries items, no more or less.

All students must have on their person two hundred dollars USA currency in denominations of twenties only, no fewer, no more. Procure these bills only from a banking institution.

All students must provide a health certificate and receive the following immunizations on attached document.

I stared at the documents. There were five back-to-back sheets attached with demands, signatures required, and releases. I wondered if this was an experience for her worth my paying for? After all, she'd been all over Europe. I felt kind of blindsided. As usual, there had been no phone call of excitement from my daughter. Did she really want to go? I knew she had a new boyfriend and that they were "really in love," would she want to leave Handsome Harry? I pondered the options, picked up the phone to call her, then hung up. I needed to think.

"Immersion" is a great buzz word used frequently by the collegiate administration to defend their demand that you let your kid have fun in college. Remember, she was "immersing" herself in her surrounding college community; having her nails manicured, sucking up two lattes a day, going to movies, and laying out in her hated pink bikini on the shores of Marina del Ray. Still, I worried that I might be denying my child a great lifetime opportunity if I didn't let her dip her toes into the soil of China as well.

So, I phoned her.

Of course, she wanted to go, was I crazy? To miss an opportunity like that?

Chagrined, I asked meekly, "What about Handsome Harry, your new boyfriend? I thought you guys were—"

"Harry and I already talked about it. He'll come out in the summer during break. They said that housing allows visitors."

Great. International shack-up—on us.

The Monday for takeoff was approaching: My daughter and I were running amok. We'd been up since six in the morning. She had a seven o'clock hair appointment, as she wanted her hair cut before she left "civilization." I was off to get the get special "color designated" luggage tags, the two-hundred dollars (remember, those twenties had to come from a bank, be "clean" with no flaws, and then placed in a zip-lock bag with clear tape on it,) and electrical converters for her hair dryer, computer, etc. Fortunately, she was almost packed, so I figured that after her hair cut, we'd have a leisurely brunch. Her boyfriend would come over for dinner and she'd kiss all the males her in life bye-bye, and we'd be up at the crack of dawn to go to the airport.

So, I had a plan, in other words, a guarantee that it will be fucked-up of course.

I was sitting in the car, nursing a cup of coffee, about to go into the bank. The phone rang.

I answered gaily, "Hello, this is M, aka Perfect Mom."

"Hello, this is Ms. Everett, I'm the travel coordinator for today's trip."

Heads-up, when she said *today's trip*, I should have levitated from the seat, but I did not.

"Err… yes, Thing Two is almost packed and we will be there early tomorrow morning."

"Well, that's just lovely, but we are leaving *today*—in about three hours"

"But, her note said *Monday*."

"Yes Mam, it's called a time zone change: She'll be arriving in *China on Monday*, but not really…. Do you understand?"

I understood that I, with my Masters, five credentials, was an idiot.

Ms. Everett continued to berate me; warning that even if we did make it to the airport, that customs might not let us through. I nodded silently as I found my car. I phoned my friend, Babs. Babs has no children therefore she is always a rational, steady, pleasant person. She immediately took control of my insanity.

"Alright M, now breathe. Okay, enough breathing. Go get Thing Two. I will get the money in crisp twenties, the chargers, the converters. I'll meet you at the house."

I was passive. I agreed and made the dreaded phone call to Thing Two at the hair salon. After my first words, "Your plane is today, not tomorrow," she was intelligible. She was screaming like a banshee. Something about not kissing Handsome

Harry and her father goodbye, and of course, what a horrible and stupid mother I was. *Why hadn't I interpreted the directions correctly?* No mention that she refused to let me re-read anything, stating that she was old enough for world travel and could "handle everything—just relax Mother and get me the stuff *you're* assigned to get."

I called Babs for additional morale support. I knew I needed her chatting so I wouldn't start drinking while driving.

"I've got the money and the converters. Pick me up. I'm going with you. You're not safe without an adult supervising you."

She and I picked up a screaming, hysterical teenager. Babs wisely sat in the back, her eyes squinting to fill out the tiny specially designated luggage tags, while fighting waves of car-sick nausea. Meanwhile, Thing Two was on her cell ranting, begging poor boyfriend to meet her at the airport, which would normally an hour drive. She called her Papa who weakly attempted to calm her down, but she could barely hear him as she was sobbing and screaming on the phone.

We arrived at the airport, dragging luggage, my holding the hand of my hysterical second child, reminding me of similar experiences when she was three. My friend wisely volunteered to park the car and no doubt, pop a couple of Xanax. The line for check in was enormous. I saw a flag waving in the air for Thing Two's travel group. The be-speckled coordinator was gesturing frantically for Thing Two to join them. I started towards my daughter, intending to drag her to the front of customs somehow. However, the TSA had different ideas. A short woman with a fierce frown stood in my way, hand on her weapon. "Lady, back into the line, or…"

Great, now I'm about to be arrested in the name of love and enabling. I sputtered out our story. She didn't register any expression except contempt. I turned, looking for my daughter. *Surely when she sees how distraught my child is, she'll relent.* No, because Handsome Harry had magically appeared. He and Thing Two were passionately making out in the line. I turned back to the agent, "Please, her whole group is there. I had to pay $4000 in advance for this trip. *Please?*" Just a glare and then she eyeballed behind me.

I shrieked at my child, "Thing Two: do you want to go to China or not?"

She came up for air and screamed, "I'm saying good-bye to Harry."

The coordinator made her way over and conferred to the TSA agent. The agent marched over to me and the PDA couple, and hissed: "Poor Mommy!"

She grabbed my child by the arm, while simultaneously dragging both of her suitcases, and added, "Stupid child!"

I waved as my daughter was yanked away. No hugs or kisses for me. I stood, frozen, watching her disappear into the crowd of privileged world travelers.

Finally, she turned to me and in an angry voice announced, "I love you Mom. Please take Harry out for lunch. He's going to be depressed."

I turned to comfort Poor Harry. He shot me a lopsided grin. "Hey Mom, sad times, eh?"

He leaned down and scooped me up into a bear hug, and waved Babs over as well, including her in his embrace.

When he pulled away from us, he grinned. "Shit, I'm starving. Can we have dum-sum?"

What-the-hell? I took the love, any way I can get it

CHAPTER FOURTEEN

I'm Not Dead Yet —Oh, wait, lemme check...

I HIT THE WEIRDEST, SCARIEST DECADE OF MY LIFE, *SIXTY*. One of my book club ladies assures me that *seventy* is so paralyzing that one needs a stiff drink each morning for about thirty days to cope. I can look in the mirror and only wince, not throw up. I cannot "wait to exhale," because I'm currently trying one of those waist-cinching corsets that supposed to force your body to reabsorb your dishonorable belly fat. Yes, there is a good deal of awesome wiggling belly fat, but not any worse than some of these Twenty Something "Twinkie" girls that I see walking around in their yoga clothes regardless of whether or not they know the *Warrior Pose*. As if there is an advantage to being able to twist yourself into a position where your head might go behind the back of your knees.

OK, yes, it could come in handy when you want jewelry, but jeez, what an effort!

I am happy to be an "older" woman, whatever that is. I have lifetime friends, and that only happens if you actually live a *lifetime* to have them.

There are some Life Questions that as a *mature woman* I must face:

When your husband trades in your awesome ass-kicking Infinity G37 for a Prius Quasi-van, is this equal to female circumcision?

Can your drooping bra fat be sucked up to recreate cleavage?

How can one reconcile missing eyebrows with chin hairs?

Samantha from Sex-In-The–City excluded, why hasn't someone invented *pubic* hair dye in various "natural colors"? I see a tremendous business opportunity here… I know that they have it in primary colors, but I'm just not ready for bright yellow *down there*—maybe when I'm seventy…

Or even worse, how do we face the heartbreak of missing patches altogether? I seem to have a kind of a disorganized Brazilian for seniors *down there*.

Age does make one have less hair to shave on one's legs—of course the spider veins cover a lot of hair…

If I chose to flirt, what type of man can I expect to flirt back? Will he look like my uncle Harry or harrier? Is the Big Bad Boy no longer a realistic option?

How does one cope with the blessing and reality-check of becoming a genuine *grandmother?* Clearly, having a grandbaby is a much better deal than being a mom. Your vagina, although in critical condition of turning into a dried leaf, is at least, intact after you lay the infant down for her nap.

After you insist that your grandbaby not call you *Granny,* can you deal with the

name *Bubbie* instead?

In order to make some sense of this aging thing, I made resolutions. Wisely, most I'm not keeping.

I was going to go hang gliding. I decided that I couldn't risk leaky bladder while clinging to the cute thirty-year-old instructor.

These questions plague me. I marinate on them while drinking Malbec. I tried pot. Nothing happened. Apparently my aged-neurons are desensitized. Hari Krishna too late.

I have noted that when the local news shows a newborn baby and then some poor women who's turning one-hundred and five the same day, that they pretty much look alike, squashed up faces with wrinkles.

My kids and hubby tell me, "M., just chill. Relax. *Chillax.*" Okay, I'm doing it!

I'm looking forward to trying hard to not try so hard, to laughing more and to well, having a life-after-child-rearing. Not that the parenting ever ends. The threat of one's grown children moving back in, is ever present fear. Just the other night Thing Two announced that she might like to move up where we lived. I foolishly asked if she had a job opportunity?

She chuckled and answered, "Oh, no worries. I'll find something. Do you still have that guest room? I'd only hang for a while…"

After she hung up, I contemplated moving the exercise equipment into that "guest" room, but then I pushed the thought away while I focused on what's on Netflix tonight.

I'm enjoying my husband now. It's cutely annoying that he fusses over the oven, stacks the dishes just so, and actually cares that the cat just barfed on the rug. While, I just don't care so much anymore. I stopped dusting twice a day and admire the dust bunnies as they float over my dusty floor. It is in fact, the age of enlightenment for us both.

Oh, and all about the love, for sure.

www.ingramcontent.com/pod-product-compliance
Lightning Source LLC
Chambersburg PA
CBHW071525040426
42452CB00008B/886